The Joy of Swift

A beginner's guide to building iOS applications

by

Alan Forbes

The Joy of Swift

Table of Contents

What is Swift?..1

   Introduction..1

   How This Book is Organized...2

      Swift Syntax...2

      Writing iOS Applications and using Xcode....................................2

      Apple Frameworks...2

   Where to get Swift 3

   What if I don't have a Mac?...3

Getting Started with Swift..5

   Launching Xcode..5

   Create a New Playground..6

Part 1: Experimenting in the Playground and Variables.............................9

   Introduction..9

   Declaring Variables and Constants...10

      Comments...10

   Specifying the Variable Type...11

   Type Inference..13

   Camel Casing...13

   Printing...13

      Mixing variables into print statements..14

Basic Operations...15

   Introduction..15

   Assignment Operator..15

   Arithmetic Operations...15

   String Concatenation..16

   Increment and Decrement Operators...16

   Compound Assignments...17

   Printing...17

      Swift 2.0..17

Strings...19

    Introduction...19

    Empty Strings..19

        IsEmpty..20

    Additional Examples..20

Control Flow...21

    Introduction...21

    Comparison Operators..22

    Loops...22

    For Loop..23

    For-In...23

        While...24

        Do... While..25

    If Statements..25

        If..25

    If ... else...25

    Switch Statement..26

    Guard Statement...27

    Ternary Conditional Operator 27

Error Handling..29

    Introduction...29

Classes..31

    Introduction...31

    Creating a Class..31

        Functions within Classes...34

    Creating an Instance of a Class...34

    Computed Properties...37

Arrays...41

    Introduction...41

    Allocating arrays 41

        Inferred Type..41

Explicit Type...42

Adding objects to arrays 42

Referencing objects in an array..42

Array subset 43

Joining arrays 43

Inserting and Removing Items...43

Constant arrays 44

Dictionaries...45

Introduction..45

Declaring a Dictionary 46

Short Form Dictionary..46

Creating an Empty Dictionary...46

Mixed Types of Keys and Values......................................47

Using a Dictionary..47

Item Count..47

isEmpty..47

Subscript Syntax..47

Adding Dictionary Items..48

Changing Dictionary Items...48

Removing Dictionary Items...48

Iterating Over a Dictionary...49

Functions..51

Introduction..51

Declaring a Function...52

No Return Value..52

Functions that return a value..53

"Throwing" An Error...53

Advanced..56

Part 2: Building iOS Applications...57

Introduction..57

iOS Devices...57

Introduction to User Interface Constraints..........................58

Creating a Simple User Interface Constraint 58
Advanced User Interface Constraints.................................60
Sizing Classes & Constraints.................................61
Introduction.................................61
Auto Layout.................................61
All Positioning Is Relative.................................62
Setting a Constraint.................................63
Writing your first iPhone App.................................65
Introduction.................................65
Description of the Application.................................65
Contrasting Visual Studio and Xcode.................................66
Outlets and Actions.................................67
Outlets.................................67
Actions.................................67
Lets Build an Application.................................68
Building the User Interface.................................72
Labels.................................72
Text Fields.................................73
Adding Buttons.................................75
Running your Program in the iOS Simulator.................................75
Link the Storyboard to Code.................................78
Creating Outlets and Actions 80
Making the Calculate Button Work.................................83
Working with Images.................................87
Introduction.................................87
Adding Images to your Project File.................................88
Using the Image Control.................................89
Search Available Controls.................................89
Adding an Image to your Application.................................90
Working with the iOS UI Controls.................................92
Introduction.................................92
Typical Controls.................................92

Create a Basic Project...94

Working with the UISlider..95

Introduction..95

Create a Slider Project...95

Add UI Elements..95

Add Outlets and Actions..96

Code the Action...97

Working with the UIDatePicker...99

Introduction..99

Create a Date Picker Project..100

Add the UI Elements...100

Add Outlets and Actions...101

Code the Action...102

On Your Own...103

Working with the Segmented Control..104

Introduction..104

Create a Segmented Control Project..105

Add the UI Elements...105

Add Outlets and Actions...107

Code the Action...108

On Your Own...110

Exercise 1:..110

Exercise 2:..110

Working with the UIWebView Control...111

Introduction..111

Create a WebUIView Control Project...112

Add the UI Elements...112

Add Outlets and Actions...113

Code the Action...114

The loadAddressURL Function 115

On Your Own...116

Saving Data between Sessions..117

Introduction..117

NSUserDefaults..117

Reading and Writing Values into NSUserDefaults............................118

Advanced Use Cases..118

    Saving an Array..119

    Reading an Array..119

Multi-Screen Applications..120

Introduction..120

Adding A Second View Controller 120

Navigation Bars and Toolbars...124

Introduction..124

    Toolbar...125

Sample Application..126

Adding A Navigation Bar control 126

Placing the Navigation Bar...127

Adding Bar Button Items..129

Adding A Toolbar...130

Keyboard Tricks...132

Introduction..132

Option 1: Touch outside a text area...132

Option 2: Hide keyboard on Return key..132

Working with Maps...134

Introduction..134

A Quick Refresher on Latitude and Longitude 134

Sample Application..135

Adding A Map Control 136

Specifying the Map Starting Location and Zoom Level.......................137

Adding Annotations in Code..140

User Annotations...142

Code..144

Geolocation...146

Introduction..146

Setup and Permissions Required!...146

   Adding the Core Location framework.......................................146

   Adding the Permission Strings..148

   Adding the CLLocatonManagerDelegate................................150

Start Coding...150

Updating viewDidLoad..151

Add a Location Manager function 154

Working with Audio...155

Introduction..155

Build the User Interface..156

Add the Media...156

import AVFoundation..157

Add Global Variables...157

Add the Actions 158

   Disable the slider control on start 158

Code the Play/Pause Button..159

Adjusting the Volume..160

Submitting an app to the Apple App store......................................161

Introduction..161

   What you Need..161

   Get ready for Rejection...162

   Launch Screen..162

   Certificates and Identifiers..162

Follow Along with Apple...162

Conclusion...163

Wrapping it up..163

Internet Resources..164

(This page is intentionally left blank so that new chapters start on right-hand pages)

1

What is Swift?

Introduction

Swift is a programming language from Apple that allows you to write iOS and OSX applications. Writing Swift code is interactive and fun, the syntax is concise yet expressive, and apps run lightning-fast. Swift is ready for your next iOS and OS X project — or for addition into your current app — because Swift code works side-by-side with Objective-C.

This book focuses on writing iOS applications but the language is the same for both platforms and you use Xcode for each, so much of what you learn in the this book is directly applicable to writing OSX applications too.

One of the great things about Swift is that is designed to be more of a 'modern' programming language, particularly as compared with Objective C. Without getting into too much irrelevant information, one example Swift's superiority is the fact that Swift eliminates entire classes of unsafe code.

In Swift, variables are always initialized before use, arrays and integers are checked for overflow, and memory is managed automatically. Syntax is tuned to make it easy to define your intent — for example, simple three-character keywords define a variable (var) or constant (let).

> Xcode is the only official development environment supported by Apple.

Even better, working with Swift is just *plain fun* too. That's what inspired me to write this book-- so you could have fun with Swift too.

Let's get started.

How This Book is Organized

There are two main sections of this book-- Swift Syntax and using Xcode.

Swift Syntax

The first section deals with the basic syntax of Swift. If you have programmed before you'll likely find it at least somewhat familiar. All of the Swift exercises designed to teach you the Swift language will be done using the Xcode playground.

The playground is a new feature in Xcode that makes writing Swift code simple and fun. It allows you to experiment with the language independent of the context of an application. Using the playground, just type a line of code and the result appears immediately.

If your code includes a loop you can watch its progress in the timeline assistant. The timeline displays the values of a changing variables in a graph, which is very cool! When you've perfected your code in the playground, simply move that code into a project.

Writing iOS Applications and using Xcode

The second section of the book deals with Xcode, Apple's integrated development environment. If you've never programmed an iOS or MacOS application, this is the part your likely to have the most trouble with so it's the part of the book we're going to spend the most time with.

Apple Frameworks

A big part of learning how to program with a new language is learning how to use its object model. For instance, to be a proficient .NET developer you need to understand the .NET framework.   Regardless of whether you program in Visual Basic or C#, the object model is consistent.

In the Apple world, the object models you'll use most are Cocoa (for Mac OS applications) and Cocoa Touch (for iOS applications). In the final section of the book we'll discuss the Apple object models.

Where to get Swift

Swift is built into Xcode starting with release 6. You can find it on the Apple web site at https://developer.apple.com/xcode/downloads/ but all it really does is redirect you to the App Store for the Mac.

So the fastest way to get started is to open the App Store on your Mac and search for **Xcode** by Apple.

What if I don't have a Mac?

Xcode is an application that is **exclusively** for the Mac, so you if you don't have one you are (almost) out of luck. I say 'almost' because there actually are ways you can *rent* a Mac over the Internet. I haven't used this service and am not affiliated with it in any way, but from the looks of it MacInCloud seems like a good solution.

If you don't have a Mac yet and aren't sure this is for you, a low-risk way to try it out can be found here:

http://www.macincloud.com/

2

Getting Started with Swift

Launching Xcode

To get started playing with Swift, the first thing you need to do is launch Xcode. There are many ways to start a program on the Mac but I'll show just one. Click on the LaunchPad icon (the one that looks like a rocket)

Once Launchpad opens you'll be presented with a list of all your installed applications. You can scroll around until you see Xcode or you can type the letter x into the search bar to narrow down the list to those applications that start with X. Once you see Xcode just click to launch it.

Create a New Playground

Now that you have Xcode running you'll be presented with a welcome screen that looks similar to this:

On the right you'll see a list of previous projects (if any) and on the left you'll have the options:

1. Get started with a playground

2. Create a new Xcode project

3. Check out an existing project

We'll select option 1: **Get started with a playground**. Xcode will ask you to name your playground. Let's name our playground Joy Chapter 2 as shown:

Next Xcode will ask you where you'd like to store your new playground. I suggest that you make a folder in your Documents folder. I called mine "Swift Playground" but you can call it whatever makes sense to you. Click Next.

If you now open Finder and look in your Documents\Swift Playground folder you'll see a new file called **Joy Chapter 2.playground** has been created.

Xcode playground projects have the extension .playground

Everything your playground needs will be stored inside the .playground file. The playground file is really a container (a zip file, perhaps?) with other files inside it. For the curious, you can right-click a .playground file and select "Show Package Contents".

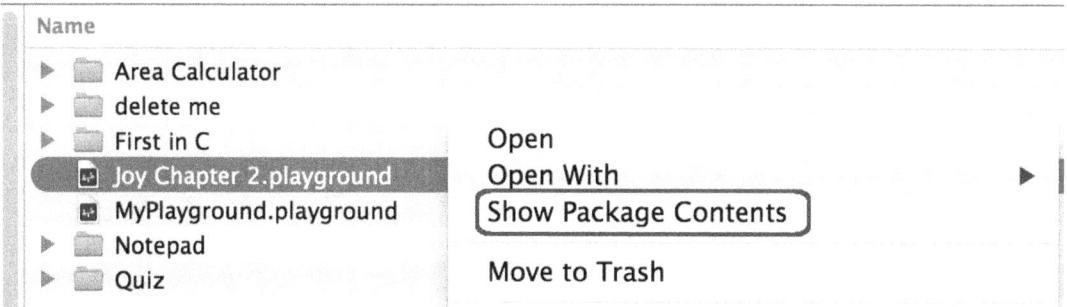

This can be useful if you want to drag images into the playground but for now let's just let it be.

3

Part 1: Experimenting in the Playground and Variables

Introduction

So now we have Xcode open in a new blank playground. Let's take a quick tour.

```
● ○ ○                    ▣ Joy Chapter 2.playground                    ⤢
▦  ◀  ▶   ▣ Joy Chapter 2.playground ⟩ No Selection

  // Playground - noun: a place where
      people can play

  import UIKit

  var str = "Hello, playground"                    "Hello, playground"
```

On the left side of the screen you see two lines of code, and on the right side of the screen you see the text "Hello, playground".   The code is:

```
import UIKit

var str = "Hello, playground"
```

The idea is that the right side of the screen gives you immediate feedback of what your program would do. Note that this program would not, in fact, output 'Hello, playground' because there is no Print statement telling the program to do this. Rather, what playground is showing you is the value of the variable **str**.

> In Swift, you declare a variable using the keyword **var**
>
> Declare a constant using the keyword **let**

The code above does one thing-- declares a variable named **str** and gives it the value "hello, playground".

Declaring Variables and Constants

In Swift, you declare a variable using the keyword **var**. You can also declare a constant (a value that once set cannot be altered) using the keyword **let**. Constants can be either strings or numbers. Here is how you declare a constant and a variable in Swift:

```
//declare a variable
var myValue = 10

//declare a constant
let pi = 3.1415

// declare multiple integers
var x = 1, y = 2, z = 3
```

Comments

The text you see above in green is a comment. (If you are reading a print version of this book or using a black & white Kindle, I'm referring to the text that starts with the two slashes. //

You can create a single-line comment by starting a line with //. If you have a lot to say, you can create mult-line comments by starting with /* then ending with */

For example

/*

This is a multi line comment.

You can never have too many comments in your code, so its a great idea to get in the habit early of putting comments into your code even in places that seem obvious to you.   I've been writing code for over 20 years and I can assure you that code I once wrote which was obvious to me was not always obvious when I went back to look at it some time later.   Comments are good.

*/

Speaking of multiples, you should also know that you can put two statements on a single line by separating them with a semi colon. For example:

```
let myName = "Alan"; print ("hello, \(myName)")
```

Personally, I think putting multiple statements on a line makes the code harder to read, but that's just my opinion.

Specifying the Variable Type

Like all programming languages, Swift offer many different types of variables such as **int** for integers, **Bool** for boolean (true/false) values, **Float** and **Double** for variables involving all but the most basic math.

If you want to be specific about what type of value a variable can hold without generating an error you can specify the type when you declare the variable by following it with a colon, then a space, then it's type as follows:

```
// declare an integer
var myInt: Int = 10
```

```
// declare a string
var myString: String = "Hello World"
```

Swift is a "Type Safe" programming language and what this means is that you can't change a variables type once it has been declared. Using the above example of **myInt**, if you subsequently set its value to 4.32 you would either get an error or an unexpected result.

In the Swift Playground, the value **myInt** would instead simply store 4 without any of the values to the right of the decimal point.

```
// declare an integer
var myInt: Int = 10                          10
myInt = 4.223                                4
```

You can also combine the declaration of multiple variables of the same time on one line as follows:

```
var north, south, east, west: String
```

Type Inference

Generally you do not have to specify the type of a variable. Swift is pretty good at figuring out ("inferring") what type a variable is. This is called "type inference".

For example, Swift will **know** that this variable is a string:

var aString = "This is a string"

Camel Casing

In general, Apple programmers tend to use something called "camel casing" when coming up with names for their variables. Camel casing is the practice of writing compound words or phrases such that each word or abbreviation begins with a capital letter. This makes it easy for the human reader to pick out the individual words, since a variable name cannot have a space in it.

In Swift the general practice is to start your variable name with a lower case letter, such as **thisIsCamelCasing**

Printing

You can print out the value of a variable in the playground using the print command. For example:

```
// declare a string
var myString: String = "Hello World"
print (myString)
```

will print out "Hello World"

```
print ("Hello World")
```

will do the same thing. You can also mix and match string constants and variables into the same print statement.

Mixing variables into print statements

You can mix a variable into a string by using a slash \ character then putting the variable name in parenthesis. For example:

```
// declare a string
var myName: String = "Alan"
print ("Hello \(myName)")
```

Basic Operations

Introduction

Like all programming languages, Swift offer many different types of operators to perform various actions. These operators include assignment, arithmetic, increment/decrement, comparison, and logic operations.

Assignment Operator

Operators used to assign or update the value of a variable or to assign the value of a constant are called "assignment operators". In Swift, the assignment operator is the equal sign (=). We have seen this one already in our previous example of

```
var myValue = 10
```

Arithmetic Operations

When it comes to arithmetic, Swift is consistent with other programming languages. Use + for addition, - for subtraction, * for multiplication and / for division. You can use these operators with all types of numbers, but beware that the type of number you use can affect the result you get.

Consider the following examples, which I encourage you to type into your own Playground:

```
5 + 2                                    7
5 - 2                                    3
5 * 2                                    10
5 / 2                                    2
5.0 / 2                                  2.5

"Hello " + "World"                       "Hello World"
|
```

Everything is what you would expect until you get to the fourth example, 5 / 2. I expect to get an answer of 2.5 when I divide 5 by 2 but Swift gave me the answer 2. Why? Swift returned 2 because it inferred the Type as Integer. I supplied Swift with 2 integers, and it gave me an integer back. To get back the expected result, you need to provide Swift with at least one floating point number.

When I ask Swift to divide 5.0 by 2 it returns 2.5. This is an easy trap to fall into!

The remainder operator is the percent sign. Thus 9 % 4 will return 1.

String Concatenation

The astute reader will notice that the last example in the above screen shot was not related to math. That's because the plus sign is so versatile. It can also be used to add two strings together. Thus, "Hello " + "World" will return "Hello World".

Increment and Decrement Operators

You can use the increment (++) operator or the decrement (--) operator to increase or decrease the value of a numeric variable by 1.

Compound Assignments

Compound assignment operators combine the assignment operator (=) with another operation, such as addition (+). Thus if you have an integer named a a and wanted to add 5 to it, you could either

a = a + 5   or a += 5

Printing

When you call the common printing functions in Swift, the value you are printing shows up in the Xcode output window.

1.   let name = "Alan"
2.   print("Hello, world")
3.   print("Hello, \(name)"

In **line 1**, I set the value of the variable name equal to my name which is Alan. In **line 2** I print the classic "Hello, world".

Finally, in **line 3** I combine the static text Hello with the value of the variable to get the output of "Hello, Alan"

Swift 2.0

Note: In Swift 2.0, the print line function (println) was dropped in favor of the simpler print.

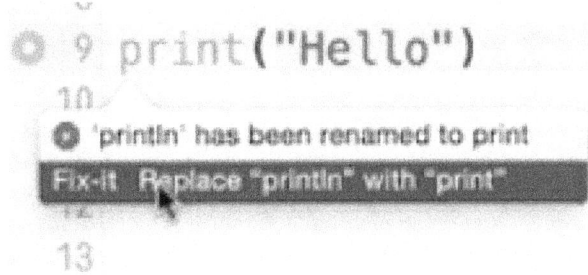

```
9 print("Hello")
10
```

5

Strings

Introduction

A *string* is an ordered collection of characters, such as `"hello, world"` or `"alan forbes"`. Swift strings are represented by the `String` type, which in turn represents a collection of values of `Character` type.

Swift's `String` and `Character` types provide a fast, Unicode-compliant way to work with text in your code. The syntax for string creation and manipulation is lightweight and readable, with a string literal syntax that is similar to C. String concatenation is as simple as adding together two strings with the `+` operator, and string mutability is managed by choosing between a constant or a variable, just like any other value in Swift.

Empty Strings

To create an empty `String` value as the starting point for building a different string, either assign an empty string to a variable

```
var emptyString = ""
```

or initialize a new `String` instance with initializer syntax:

```
var anotherEmptyString = String()
```

These two strings are both empty and entirely equivalent to each other. It is just a matter of preference as to which way you might prefer.

IsEmpty

You can find out whether a `String` value is empty by checking its boolean `isEmpty` property:

```
var emptyString = ""
if emptyString.isEmpty {
print("The string is empty")
}
```

Additional Examples

```
var myString = "Hello"
let myConstantString = " !"
myString += " World"
myString = myString + myConstantString // abc

let count = 7
let message = "There are \(count) days in a week"
let name = "Alan"
print("Hello")
print("My name is \(name)")
```

6

Control Flow

Introduction

Control flow refers to a programming statement whose execution results in a choice being made as to which of two or more paths should be followed.

The kinds of control flow statements supported by different languages vary, but can be categorized by their effect:

1. Continuation at a different statement without condition, such as the command GOTO found in BASIC

2. Executing a set of statements only if some condition is met, such as the IF statement found in virtually every programming language, including Swift

3. Executing a set of statements zero or more times, until some condition is met (i.e., loop - the same as conditional branch)

4. Executing a set of distant statements, after which the flow of control returns to the calling line, such as subroutines and functions

5. Stopping the program entirely to prevent any further execution or stopping midway through a function if a certain condition is met.

Swift provides all the familiar control flow statements you might expect if you've worked with other languages. These include **for** and **while** loops to perform a task multiple times; **if** and **switch** statements to execute different branches of code based on certain conditions; and statements such as **break** and **continue** to transfer the flow of execution to another point in your code.

Comparison Operators

Typically when you are programming a control flow operation you want to take an action only if a certain condition is met. Perhaps you want to take a different action if the condition is not met or if a different condition is met.

This implies that there is a way to test for a condition using comparison operators. Swift support the following comparison operators to represent equal to, not equal to, less than, greater than, less than or equal to, and greater than or equal to, respectively:

==, !=, <, >, <=, >=

NOTE: You use a single equal sign to assign a value, such as a = 12 and use two equal signs to test for equality, such as if a == 12. Note you need a space on either side of the operator in Swift. Other languages use a single equal sign for both operations but once you get used to using two equal signs it is much clearer.

Swift also provides for the case of three equal signs (=== and !==), which you use to test whether two object references both refer to the same object instance.

Loops

Swift provides two kinds of loop that perform a set of statements a certain number of times:

The **for** loop performs a set of statements until a specific condition is met, typically by incrementing a counter each time the loop ends.

The **for-in** loop performs a set of statements for each item in a range, sequence, collection, or progression.

For Loop

A **for** statement allows for a block of code to be repeatedly executed as long as a condition is true. With each loop, a counter is incremented. The **for** loop takes the following form in Swift:

```
for initialization; condition; increment
{
// statements
}
```

The following example will print the numbers from 1 to 5

```
for counter = 1; counter <= 5; counter++
{
   print(counter)
}
```

For-In

You use the **for-in** loop to iterate over collections of items, such as ranges of numbers, items in an array, or characters in a string.

The **for-in** loop takes the following form in Swift:

```
for instance in collection
{
// each loop gives you an instance of each object in the
colleciton
}
```

This example prints the first few entries in the two-times-table:

```
for index in 1...5 {
   print("The index value is \(index)")
```

```
print("\(index) times 2 is \(index * 2)")
}
```

The collection of items being iterated is a closed range of numbers from 1 to 5 inclusive (including both ends), as indicated by the use of the closed range operator (...). You could have also used the "half open" range format of 1..<5 if you wanted to iterate from 1 to 4.

The value of index is set to the first number in the range (1), and the statements inside the loop are executed. In this case, the loop contains two statements, the first of which prints the value of the variable index and the second of prints the current value of index multiplied by two.

After the statement is executed, the value of index is updated to contain the second value in the range (2), and the two statements are called again. This process continues until the end of the range is reached.

In the example above, *index* is a variable whose value is automatically set at the start of each iteration of the loop. It does not have to be declared before it is used. Rather, it is implicitly declared simply by being part of the loop declaration without the need for a let declaration keyword.

The **print()** statement prints a string. In this case we want to print both a string and a number. To convert the number into a string, Swift uses the convention of \(number).

While

A while loop executes as long as condition is true (while true). This type of loop evaluates the expression first, and if the condition is true then the code is executed.

```
// while loop
var i = 1
while i < 1000 {
  i *= 2
```

```
}
```

Do... While

This variation of the while loop is called the do...while loop. It executes the code at least once, then evaluates the condition to decide whether or not to execute it again.

```
// do-while loop
do {
  print("hello")
} while 1 == 2
```

If Statements

If

An **if** statement takes the simple case of if a condition is true, then perform the conditional code, as shown:

```
if condition
{
answer1
}
```

In the case of an **if** statement, no code is guaranteed to run. Either the code block executes or it does not.

If ... else

An **if..else** statement differs slightly from an if statement in that two blocks of code are provided and either one or the other will be executed depending on the value of the condition. It takes the form of "if the condition is true, then do the first thing, otherwise do the second thing".

```
if condition
{
first thing
}
else
{
second thing
}
```

Switch Statement

The **switch** statement allows your program to select one of several options based on a value. For instance if you were writing a program for the local fire station you might code something like this:

```
1.    let alertLevel = "Elevated"
2.
3.    switch alertLevel {
4.    case "Low" :
5.       print ("Not much danger of fires today.")
6.    case "High" :
7.       print ("Be careful today.")
8.    case "Elevated" :
9.       print ("No campfires allowed today.  The danger is great."
10.   default :
11.      print ("You should be careful regardless of the conditions.")
```

Swift will execute the code where the variable following the word switch contains the value following the word **case**. In the above example the variable **alertLevel** contains the value "Elevated" – this was set in **Line 1**. The match for this is found on **Line 8**, so the code on **Line 9** will be executed. If no match is found, the code following the keyword **default** will be executed instead.

Guard Statement

New to Swift 2.0 is the **guard** statement. The **guard** statement is similar to an if statement in that it allows you to execute code if a boolean condition is met. But it basically works the opposite of an if. With guard the else block is required. In fact the else block is the *point* of the guard statement. The only values the else can take are return, break, continue, or throw.

```
guard condition else {return/break/continue/throw}
```

Assuming that your else block contains either return or break, the guard checks a condition and **exits** if the condition is not met. If the condition *is* met, the lines following guard are executed. (The opposite is true if your else block is continue, of course.

If you are going to use guard to exit or continue, it only makes sense that guard can only be used in a place where exiting or continuing is possible, such as within a loop or in a function. The following code should be entered into a playground to try out.

```
func helloWorld(){
let myWords ="Hello World"
guard myWords.characters.count > 5 else {return}
print (myWords)
}
helloWorld()
```

Ternary Conditional Operator

A ternary conditional operator is a special operator with three parts, which takes the form:

condition ? trueAnswer : falseAnswer

It is a shortcut way of writing an **if..else** statement. The format is if condition is true: trueAnswer, if question is false: falseAnswer.

In my opinion this style of programming is **much** harder to read for not much gain.

7

Error Handling

Introduction

All code occasionally produces an error. Error handling refers to the anticipation, detection, and resolution of errors related to programming or unanticipated conditions.

The way to handle errors in Swift is to use the do / try / catch syntax.

```
do {
    //execute code here using the try statement
}
catch
{
    //catch and handle the error here
}
```

Here's an example

```
do {
    //execute code here using the try statement
    let myName = try "Alan"
}
catch
```

```
{
//catch and handle the error here
print ("I encountered an error")
}
```

OK so that wasn't *much* of a real-world example because we know that a simple string assignment will work but the point was to show the syntax. This example is *not* going to produce an error, but if you were setting myName by calling a function, or searching for a file you might well get an error.

Classes

Introduction

Classes are general-purpose constructs that become the building blocks of your program's code. You can define properties and methods to add functionality to your classes by using exactly the same syntax as for constants, variables, and functions. You cannot use a class directly. Rather, you define a class then create instances of it.

An instance of a class is traditionally known as an object.

One of the surprisingly useful things about classes is that one class can inherit from another. I'll try to explain that further once we understand what a class is.

Creating a Class

The convention is to start the name of your class with a capital letter. Here's a basic class definition.

```
class ClassName {
    // code here
}
```

Inside a class you can store variables and also define functions. If you were a used car dealer, you might want to define a class of **Automobile** then create instances of that class to keep track of individual cars you have for sale.

When you create *instances* of a class, each instance is separate. For example you can define variables for VIN (vehicle identification number), make, model, and price in your class. Of course, each used car on your lot would have it's own VIN, price, and make and model.

Let's see how we could implement such a class in code:

```
1.      class Automobile {
2.          init(){
3.             print ("Car created")
4.          }
5.          var Make: String = ""
6.          var Model: String = ""
7.          var Price: Double = 0
8.
9.          func bestPrice() -> Double {
10.            let myPrice = Price * 0.9
11.            return myPrice
12.         }
13.     }
14.
15.     var  car1 = Automobile ()
16.     car1.Make = "Ford"
17.     car1.Model = "Explorer"
18.     car1.Price = 20000
19.     print (car1.Make, car1.Model)
20.     print ("The best price is ", car1.bestPrice())
21.
22.     var car2 = Automobile()
23.     car2.Make = "Toyota"
24.     car2.Model = "4Runner"
25.     car2.Price = 29000
26.     print (car2.Make, car2.Model)
```

27.   print ("The best price is ", car2.bestPrice())

Line 1 declares the class. The start of the class has an opening bracket { and the end of the class is indicated by } which is on **Line 13**.

The first thing we do is initialize the class. *Initialization* is the process of preparing an instance of a class for use. This process involves setting an initial value for each stored property on that instance and performing any other setup that may be required before the new instance is ready for use.

You define the initialization by declaring an **init** function. If init takes parameters, then you will need to provide these parameters when creating an instance of the class. For example, if the value of the VIN is set during initialization, you would declare it as:

init (VIN: string) {

For purposes of keeping it simple, our example does not require parameters to init, thus **Line 2** reads simply init(){

```
init(){
    print ("Car created")
}
```

In our example, init begins on **Line 2** and ends on **Line 4**. The only code that is executed during our initialization is **Line 3** which prints out "Car created".

```
var Make: String = ""
var Model: String = ""
var Price: Double = 0
```

Lines 5 – 7 create some variables that the class can use, and sets their initial values. Swift will not allow stored properties to be left in an indeterminate state.   You can set an initial value for a stored property within an initializer or by assigning a default property value as part of the property's definition.   In our example, we set the default value as part of the property's definition. But we could also have done it like this:

```
init(){
    print ("Car created")
```

```
        Make = ""
    }
```

Functions within Classes

Classes can contain more than just variables, they can also contain functions. Our example Automobile class has one function-- **bestPrice**. The point of the function is to tell the salesperson what is the best price that they could accept if offered by the buyer.

Our example is a simple one, but you can imagine that at a real car dealership the calculation could be quite complex and take into account how long the car has been on the lot and how much interest the dealership has paid while it has been sitting there. In our example, we've decided that as long as the buyer offers at least 90% of the asking price, we have a deal. **Lines 9 – 12** implement this logic, repeated below for convenience:

```
    func bestPrice() -> Double {
        let myPrice = Price * 0.9
        return myPrice
    }
```

Finally, **Line 13** ends the class definition with a closing curly brace.

Creating an Instance of a Class

Next we're going to use our class. This is done in **Lines 15 – 27** of the original code block.   To make it easier to follow, I have repeated it below and restarted the numbering.

```
1.    var  car1 = Automobile ()
2.    car1.Make = "Ford"
3.    car1.Model = "Explorer"
4.    car1.Price = 20000
5.    print (car1.Make, car1.Model)
6.    print ("The best price is ", car1.bestPrice())
```

```
7.
8.     var car2 = Automobile()
9.     car2.Make = "Toyota"
10.    car2.Model = "4Runner"
11.    car2.Price = 29000
12.    print (car2.Make, car2.Model)
13.    print ("The best price is ", car2.bestPrice())
```

You'll notice that the code is in two similar blocks. This is because I created two instances of the class-- one to track a *Ford Explorer* and one to track a *Toyota 4Runner*.

We create an instance of class with the first line in the block, found on **Line 1** and a second instance of the class on **Line 8**.

```
var  car1 = Automobile ()
```

The lines that follow assign values to the variables associated with each class instance, such as:

```
car1.Make = "Ford"
car1.Model = "Explorer"
car1.Price = 20000
```

car1's **Make** is set to Ford on **Line 2** while car2's **Make** is set to Toyota on **Line 9**.   While both instances have a Make, Swift keeps them entirely separate. We refer to the instances using the object name, then a dot, then the variable name, such as car2.Make. This is called dot notation.

Finally, I give examples of how to **retrieve** the variables, and how to call a function. To retrieve the variable values we can use the same dot notation we used to set the value. For instance:

```
print (car2.Make)
```

Calling a function works the exact same way.

```
car2.bestPrice()
```

The last line of the block prints out the best price like this:

print ("The best price is ", car2.bestPrice())

```
//: Playground - noun: a place where people can play

import UIKit

class Automobile {
    init(){
        print ("Car created")                             (2 times)
    }
    var Make: String = ""
    var Model: String = ""
    var VIN: String = ""
    var Price: Double = 0

    func bestPrice() -> Double {
        let myPrice = Price * 0.9                          (2 times)
        return myPrice                                     (2 times)

    }
}

var  car1 = Automobile ()                                  Automobile
car1.Make = "Ford"                                         Automobile
car1.Model = "Explorer"                                    Automobile
car1.Price = 20000                                         Automobile
print (car1.Make, car1.Model)                              "Ford Explorer\n"
print ("The best price is ", car1.bestPrice())            "The best price is  18000.0\n"

var car2 = Automobile()                                    Automobile
car2.Make = "Toyota"                                       Automobile
car2.Model = "4Runner"                                     Automobile
car2.Price = 29000                                         Automobile
print (car2.Make, car2.Model)                              "Toyota 4Runner\n"
print ("The best price is ", car2.bestPrice())|           "The best price is  26100.0\n"
```

Computed Properties

A computed property is similar in behavior to a function. Continuing with our Automobile class example, an alternate way of implementing our bestPrice logic would be to define it as a computed property.

```
var bestPrice: Double {
get {
      return Price * 0.9
      }
)
```

This means that you can "get" the bestPrice of an automobile just be referring to its bestPrice property.

Computed properties can also be **set**. For example, if Model were a computed property then we could automatically set the Make in some cases. Here's an example:

```
var Make: string {
set {
      if Make == "Explorer" {
      Model = "Ford"
   }
)
```


The code above won't run as is because if a computed property has a set it must also have a get but that's the basic idea. Here is the entire example tweaked to use computed properties rather than a function:

```
1.    //: Example of computed property
2.    class Automobile {
3.        private var myModel: String = ""
4.
5.        init(){
6.            print ("Car created")
```

```
7.        }
8.        var Model: String {
9.          set {
10.             myModel = Model
11.             if Model == "Explorer" {
12.                 Make = "Ford"
13.                 }
14.           }
15.          get {
16.             return myModel

18.           }
19.        }
20.
21.        var Make: String = ""
22.        var VIN: String = ""
23.        var Price: Double = 0
24.
25.        var bestPrice: Double {
26.        get {
27.            return Price * 0.9
28.        }
29.        }
30.
31.    }
32.
33.    var  car1 = Automobile ()
34.    //car1.Make = "Ford"
35.    car1.Model = "Explorer"
36.    car1.Price = 20000
37.    print (car1.Make, car1.Model)
38.    print ("The best price is ", car1.bestPrice)
```

There are a couple of changes to note. On **Line 3** I declare a private variable called myModel. Adding private to the variable declaration means that it cannot be used outside the class. I need this variable to store the value of the model of the automobile. But don't I *already* have this you wonder? Not quite.

I want to run code whenever the value of Model is set. A rule in Swift is that you cannot have a **set** without also having a **get**.

I don't want to manipulate the value of Model-- just Make-- but Swift won't let **get** return itself. So to get around this I created a private variable that gets set on **Line 10** when Model is set and returned on **Line 16** when Model is retrieved by the get function.

Line 34 which previously set the value of Make to "Ford" is now commented out but Make still gets set to Ford by virtue of the code inside the setter for Model.   Pretty slick, isn't it?

Line 25 implements bestPrice as a computed variable which only has a get. The same logic as before is implemented-- 90% of the asking price.

On **Line 38** you might notice that now I call bestPrice just like any other variable whereas in the previous example I had to call it by passing parameters (even though no parameters are required) by following bestPlan with parenthesis, as bestPrice().

Arrays

Introduction

Arrays are a collection of data items that can be selected by indices computed at run-time. Arrays allow fast memory access to primitive data types, language objects, and custom objects.

Allocating arrays

To allocate an empty array, use the following syntax:

```
var myArray = Int[]()
```

Arrays in Swift are typed and this means that when creating an array you must specify the data types that will be inserted into the array. The array above will hold integers.

Inferred Type

Swift will infer the type if you allocate an array and initialize it with objects in the same line but otherwise the type must be explicitly specified.

To allocate an array with an inferred type, use this syntax:

```
var myArray = [1, 2, 3, 4, 5]
```

Explicit Type

You can still use the static typing when allocating and initializing your arrays, like this:

```
var myArray: Int[] = [1, 2, 3, 4, 5]
```

Adding objects to arrays

Adding objects to arrays is very easy. You can use the overloaded + operator to easily add a new object to an existing array, as follows:

```
var myArray = ["Hello"]
var myString: String = "World"
myArray += myString
```

Once you use the + operator, the myString object will be automagically written to the array, and the myArray array will now have "World" as the second object.

Referencing objects in an array

To access an object in the array you need a way to reference it. Consider the following scenario:

```
var myArray = ["Hello", "World"]
```

If you want to replace the second object in that array (the "World" string) with "Alan," you can do the following:

```
myArray[1] = "Alan"
```

In the brackets, place the index (number) of the item that you'd like to work with. The array index starts with 0 and counts up so the second object is at index 1 and not 2.

Array subset

If you need to access a subset of the items in an array you can do that using Swift's range features. To get a particular range of objects and place it into an entirely new array that contains a subset, as follows:

```
var myArray = ["One", "Two", "Three", "Four", "Five"]
var subsetArray = myArray[0..2]
```

Using the two dots between the two numbers representing the range means to start at index 0 and include all objects in indexes up to but not including index 2.

If you wish to include the object represented by the last number in the range, you'll want to do this instead:

```
var myArray = ["One", "Two", "Three", "Four", "Five"]
var subsetArray = myArray[0...2]
```

The subtle difference of using **three dots** instead of two means that you want to include the final object at that index.

Joining arrays

Joining arrays, like adding objects to the array, is very easy. Again, you'll use the + operator to join two different arrays. Let's take a look at this example:

```
var myFirstArray = ["One", "Two", "Three", "Four", "Five"]
var mySecondArray = ["Six", "Seven", "Eight", "Nine", "Ten"]
myFirstArray += mySecondArray
```

After doing this, the first array (myFirstArray) will contain ten items-- the written representation of digits from one to ten.

Inserting and Removing Items

To remove items from an array you use the **removeAtIndex** method.

```
var myArray = ["One", "Two", "Three", "Four", "Five"]
myArray.removeAtIndex(4)
```

After executing this code the myArrary will hold One, Two, Three, and Four.

To insert an item into the array use the insert method. This method takes a parameter to specify where to insert the item.

```
var days = ["Monday", "Thursday"]
var firstDay = days[0] // Monday
days.insert("Tuesday", atIndex: 1) // [Monday, Tuesday,
Thursday]
days[2] = "Wednesday" // [Monday, Tuesday, Wednesday]
days.removeAtIndex(0) // [Tuesday, Wednesday]
```

Constant arrays

If you define an array as a constant you cannot change the size of the array by adding or removing items. Declare the array as a constant by using the let command, as follows

```
let myArray = ["One", "Two", "Three", "Four", "Five"]
```

You *can* modify the **contents** of a particular index in the array if it already exists.

```
myArray[2] = "Three and a half" // this is OK
```

10

Dictionaries

Introduction

A dictionary is a type of data structure that stores multiple values of the same type. Each value is associated with a unique key, which acts as an identifier for that value within the dictionary.

Unlike items in an array, items in a dictionary do not have a specific order. You can use a dictionary when you need to look up values based on their identifier, in much the same way that a real-world dictionary is used to look up the definition for a particular word.

A key-value pair is a combination of a key and a value. When defining a dictionary the key and value in each key-value pair are separated by a colon. The key-value pairs are written as a list, separated by commas, surrounded by a pair of square brackets:

A Dictionary is a collection of keys and values, such as

[key 1: value 1, key 2: value 2, key 3: value 3]

Declaring a Dictionary

The example below creates a dictionary to store the names of international airports. In this dictionary, the keys are the three-letter International Air Transport Association codes, and the values are the actual airport names:

```swift
var airports: [String: String] = ["BOS": "Boston Logan",
"DUB": "Dublin", "MCO": "Orlando", "LAX": "Los Angeles
International", "NCE": "Nice France"]
```

The **airports** dictionary is declared as having a type of [String: String], which means "a Dictionary whose keys are of type String, and whose values are also of type String".

This is not the only combination of keys and values, however. See the following section **Mixed Types of Keys and Values**.

Short Form Dictionary

You don't have to write the type of the dictionary if you are initializing it with a dictionary literal whose keys and values have consistent types. The initialization of airports could have been be written in a shorter form instead:

```swift
var airports = ["BOS": "Boston", "DUB": "Dublin", "MCO":
"Orlando", "LAX": "Los Angeles", "NCE": "Nice France"]
```

Because all keys in the literal are of the same type as each other, and likewise all values are of the same type as each other, Swift can infer that [String: String] is the correct type to use for the airports dictionary.

Creating an Empty Dictionary

As with arrays, you can create an empty Dictionary of a certain type by using the initializer syntax:

```swift
var airports = [String: String]()
```

Mixed Types of Keys and Values

In the previous example of the airport dictionary we specified both the key and the value in the dictionary be of type string. But this is not the only way that dictionaries can be used.

```
var namesOfIntegers = [1: "One", 2: "Two", 3: "Three"]
```

Using a Dictionary

You access and modify a dictionary through its methods and properties, or by using the subscript syntax which will be explained shortly.

Item Count

As with an array, you can find out the number of items in a Dictionary by checking its read-only **count** property:

```
print("The integers dictionary contains \
(namesOfIntegers.count) items.")
```

isEmpty

Use the Boolean isEmpty property as a shortcut for checking whether the count property is equal to 0:

```
if airports.isEmpty {
print("The airports dictionary is empty.")
}
```

Subscript Syntax

You can refer to items in the dictionary and even add a new item to a dictionary with the subscript syntax.

Adding Dictionary Items

Use a new key of the appropriate type as the subscript index, and assign a new value of the appropriate type:

```
namesOfIntegers[4] = "Four"
```

Changing Dictionary Items

You can also use subscript syntax to change the value associated with a particular key:

```
airports["BOS"] = "Boston Logan"
```

Executing the above code with change the value for "BOS" to "Boston Logan"

Removing Dictionary Items

You can use subscript syntax to remove a key-value pair from a dictionary by assigning a value of `nil` for that key:

```
airports["AF"] = "Alan Forbes International"
airports["AF"] = nil
```

"Alan Forbes International" is not yet a real airport, so go ahead and delete that one from your dictionary.

Iterating Over a Dictionary

You can easily iterate over all the key-value pairs in a dictionary with a for-in loop. Each item in the dictionary is returned as a (key, value) tuple, and you can decompose the tuple's members into temporary constants or variables as part of the iteration:

```
for (airportCode, airportName) in airports {
print("\(airportCode): \(airportName)")
}
```

Swift's `Dictionary` type is an unordered collection. The order in which keys, values, and key-value pairs are retrieved when iterating over a dictionary is not necessarily what you expect.

11

Functions

Introduction

Functions are self-contained chunks of code that perform a specific task. When creating a function, you give it a name that identifies what it does, and this name is used to "call" the function to perform its task when needed.

The primary benefit of functions is in the case where a particular operation needs to be performed multiple times, perhaps from multiple places in your code. Rather than repeat code throughout your program, you just write a function and call it whenever you need it.

Swift's function syntax is flexible enough to express anything from a simple function with no parameters to a complex method with multiple parameters. Parameters can provide default values to simplify function calls and can be passed "by reference", which allows the function to modify a passed variable once the function has completed its execution.

Declaring a Function

No Return Value

If your function doesn't have a return value, you can just define the function with no type. Functions with no return type technically return "Void" but there is no need to specify this nor really worry about it.

An example of a function that does not have a return value would be one that writes a message into a log file. Assume that at various places in your program you would like to write certain messages into a text file that you will review after a run to help you figure out what the program is doing and how long each block of code took to execute. This would involve opening a text file for writing (creating it if it doesn't exist), appending a new line to the end of the file, writing a time/date stamp followed by a space, writing your message, and then closing the file.

This is code you would **not** want to repeat in multiple places so it would make sense to create a function to perform this operation. Once you had a function, all you would have to do each time you wanted a log entry is call the function with the message you want written to the log.

This function would not have a return value because it is not manipulating the message in any way, it is just writing it to the log.

You declare a simple function that does not have a return value using the following syntax:

```
func functionName (parameterName:parameterType)
{
//Code to execute ...
{
```

To create a function that writes to a log you might have something like:

```
func writeLogEntry (message:String)
{
//Code that writes the log here ...
```

```
{
```
Functions that return a value

Sometimes you need a function that **does** return a value. For example, assume you are making a weather-related application. The user provides a list of favorite cities and your program will display the current temperature for those cities. If the user provides 10 cities, you'll need to perform this look up 10 times. A function that takes a city name and returns the current temperature might look like this:

```
func cityTemperature (city:String)  -> Double
{
//Code that gets the temperature here ...
{
```

Declaring the return types at the end of a function definition (following the ->) is a fairly significant change for Apple but it will seem familiar to programmers of other languages, such as Visual Basic.

"Throwing" An Error

Functions are used to calculate a value of some kind occasionally run into trouble. Although we as programmers try to anticipate all that can happen in our program, it does not always work that way.

Keeping on the example above, what happens if sometime in the future a new programmer takes over your code and calls the cityTemperature function but passes it a city name that the function does not recognize? Should the function return a specific number that indicates "not found"?

The better practice would be to have the function "throw" an error. I like to picture that a program throwing an error is like a 4 year old throwing a fit. Basically it didn't get what it wants so mayhem ensues unless you handle it properly.

To build error handling into a function you need to tweak the function a bit. On the opening line on which you declare a function, you add the word "throws" before the return type which tells the compiler that this function is **capable** of throwing an error:

```
func cityTemperature (city:String)  throws -> Double
{
//Code that gets the temperature here ...
}
```

Of course we haven't yet specified in which cases an error will be thrown, so let's do that next. First, you need to declare the types of errors that the function can throw. You do this by defining an enum of type ErrorType.

I'll create two types of errors: 1) that the city was not found, and 2) that I have no data for the city requested.

```
enum cityError: ErrorType {
    case NotFound
    case NoData
}
```

Let's fill in the skeleton of the cityTemperature function:

```
func cityTemperature (city:String) throws -> Double
{
    if city == "Boston"{
       return 70}
    else
    {
       throw cityError.NotFound
    }
}
```

It's not much of a function. If you pass the function the value "Boston" it will return the number 70, otherwise it will throw a city not found error.

Next you need to call that function, and code for the possibility that the function will return an error:

Let's create another function which uses cityTemperature:

```
1.    func printErrors() {
2.        do {
3.            var temp: Double
4.            temp = try cityTemperature("Boston")
5.            print (temp)
6.        }
7.        catch cityError.NotFound{
8.            print ("Sorry I don't know that city.")
9.        }
10.       catch {
11.           print ("Some other error occurred.")
12.       }
13.   }
```

To use error handling, first put the whole thing in a **do** block. **Line 2** opens the do block and **Line 6** closes it. The code inside the do block is what we're supposed to do if everything goes OK On **Line 3** I declare a variable called **temp** (for temperature, not temporary) which will be of type Double.

One **Line 4** I set the value of temp equal to the value returned by the **cityTemperature** function, which in turn was passed the parameter "Boston" – the name of the city for which I would like the temperature. What's important about **Line 4** is that I don't just set the value, I **try** to set the value. Instead of:

temp = cityTemperature("Boston")

I call it this way:

temp = **try** cityTemperature("Boston")

If there is some problem setting temp, I want to handle or "catch" the error. On **Line 7** I handle the case where the city name is not known to the function. It specifically only handles one type of error – cityError.NotFound – which is the error type specified after the word catch. Change the code on **Line 4** yourself to some city other than Boston and you'll see this error get handled gracefully.

Maybe some other kind of error might occur too. On **Line 10** I handle that possibility. **Line 10** merely states **catch**, which means execute this code if you get an error this has not already been explicitly handled. I don't specifically handle the **NoData** error type specified in my cityError enums. I don't have to because the generic catch will handle it.

In addition to handling the error types you know about and can reasonably anticipate, it's also important to handle the ones you don't expect with a universal catch statement. This way if a function changes the set of errors it throws in the future, callers of that function will still catch its errors.

Advanced

If you really want to get advanced, although it is beyond the scope of this book, every function in Swift has at least one type: the function's parameter types and its return type. You can use these types like any other type in Swift, which makes it easy to pass functions as parameters to other functions, and to return functions from functions.

12

Part 2: Building iOS Applications

Introduction

iOS (known previously as "iPhone OS)" is a mobile operating system developed by Apple Inc. and runs exclusively on Apple hardware.

The user interface of iOS is based on the concept of direct manipulation using multi-touch gestures. Interface control elements consist of sliders, switches, and buttons. Interaction with the OS includes gestures such as swipe, tap, pinch, and reverse pinch, all of which have specific meanings within the context of the operating system.

iOS shares with OS X some frameworks such as Core Foundation and Foundation; however, its UI toolkit is **Cocoa Touch** rather than OS X's **Cocoa**, so that it provides the UIKit framework rather than the AppKit framework. Because iOS uses a different UI framework as Apple's Mac operating system (OS X), it is not compatible with OS X for applications.

Major versions of iOS are typically released annually.

iOS Devices

Apple has produced a wide variety of devices that utilize iOS including several variations the iPod Touch, iPad, and iPhone.

As of this writing, there have been ten major releases of iPhone (original iPhone, iPhone 3G, iPhone 3GS, iPhone 4, iPhone 4S, iPhone 5, iPhone 5C, iPhone 5S, iPhone 6, and iPhone 6 Plus), five of iPod Touch, six of iPad (first generation, iPad 2, third and fourth generations, iPad Air, and iPad Air 2), and three of iPad Mini (first generation, iPad Mini 2, and iPad Mini 3).

That's quite a collection of devices!

Introduction to User Interface Constraints

User interface constraints are critical to creating applications that run consistently across the various iOS devices. These different devices feature different screen resolutions with the more recent devices generally having a higher resolution than the generation before it. As if that's not enough, internal accelerometers are used by some applications to allow for easy rotation from portrait to landscape mode.

What this means to the developer is that if you place a button to appear in the center of the screen on an iPhone 4 it will be off-center on an iPhone 5. If you place it to be centered on an iPhone 6 screen in might not even be visible on an iPod Touch.

User Interface Constraints are the solution to this problem. User Interface Constraints allow you set constraints that define where a specific element should appear. In short, when you add elements to the screen some constraints are created automatically and will automatically space your items. Others are not automatically constrained so you must create them by selecting an element and using the size inspector or pin constraints to prevent collisions and allow rotation to automatically re-position elements.

Creating a Simple User Interface Constraint

Imagine a simple application with nothing more than a text label you wish to display centered on the screen, regardless of device type and orientation.

Start off by creating a new Single View Application for iOS in Xcode. Click on the link labeled Main.Storyboard to display the storyboard on the screen.

Next, click the link at the bottom of the screen that says w**Any** h**Any**. Move your mouse until you have one column and two rows selected, as shown below:

Hello World!

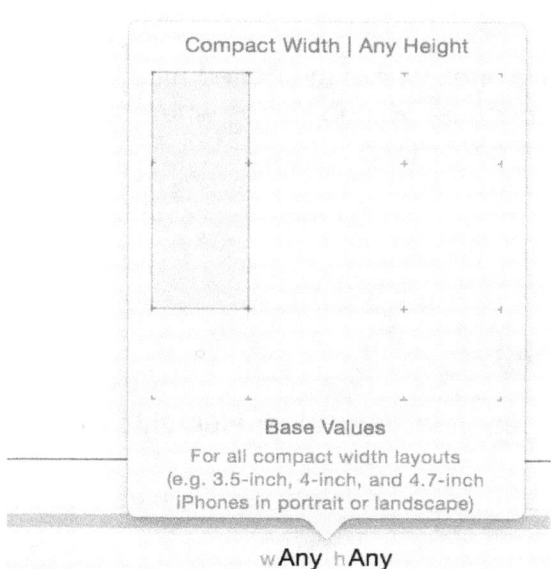

Drag a label into the center of the screen. You'll know the label is centered when the two blue lines appear as shown:

Next click the little icon in the bottom right hand corner that looks like this:

A menu will pop up from which you select 'Add Missing Constraints'

All Views in View Controller
  Update Frames
  Update Constraints
  Add Missing Constraints
  Reset to Suggested Constraints
  Clear Constraints

Once this is done you should see solid lines where the dotted blue lines used to be. This simple example will work because Xcode knows where to place the label because it's obvious that you centered it.

Other placements aren't so simple and require a bit more work on your part which we'll discuss in the next section.

Advanced User Interface Constraints

Sometimes you want elements to appear relative to other elements. This is discussed in the next chapter.

13

Sizing Classes & Constraints

Introduction

With the proliferation of Apple devices comes a proliferation of screen sizes. The iPad, iPad mini, iPhone 5, iPhone 6, and iPhone 6 Plus all have different screen resolutions.

Auto Layout

Auto Layout is Apple's approach to building responsive applications. Responsive means that that the design will resize for (or respond to) different screens.

When working in the Story Board, click on the text in the bottom center that usually says "Any / Any" as shown below:

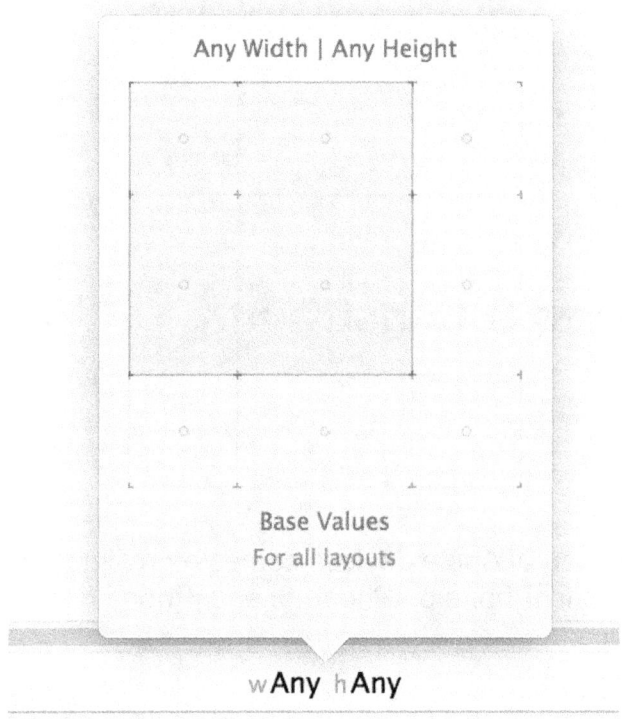

Any Width | Any Height

Base Values
For all layouts

w **Any** h **Any**

To set your storyboard to the approximate size of an iPhone, set the **w Compact, h Any**

This is a hard thing to explain in words but I will give it my best shot and recommend some youtube videos at the end of the chapter.

All Positioning Is Relative

The trick to getting UI elements to appear where you want them to appear is to tell Xcode where the element should go relative to the edges of the screen, or relative to another element which Xcode knows how to place.

For example, let's assume you had two buttons and you wanted them to be centered horizontally near the top of the screen, with one on top of the other.

First you would need to tell Xcode that the first button should be centered, and a certain distance from the top of the screen. Next you would tell Xcode that the second button should be a certain distance below the first button.

Setting a Constraint

The way that you tell Xcode where elements should go is to select them then press and hold the control key while you drag the mouse to the item you want the current item to be positioned relative to.

For example, drag to the top of the View Controller or to the side of the View Controller or to another UI element. When you drag from an element to another, Xcode asks you how you want to position it.

14

Writing your first iPhone App

Introduction

We're going to start off building a very simple iPhone app. The app will compute a hotel bill based on the number of nights stayed and the room rate. It's going to multiply two numbers together and put the result into a label.

Now this may not seem like much of an app, and in fairness it isn't. As they say, you have walk before you can run. So let's walk.

Description of the Application

The application will have a label at the top that says "Hotel Bill Calculator". It will also have two labels and two input boxes, for number of nights and the room rate. It will have a button labeled 'Calculate' and a text area at the bottom that shows the total.

Here is a youtube video describing the application:
https://www.youtube.com/watch?v=OhViluOnmg8

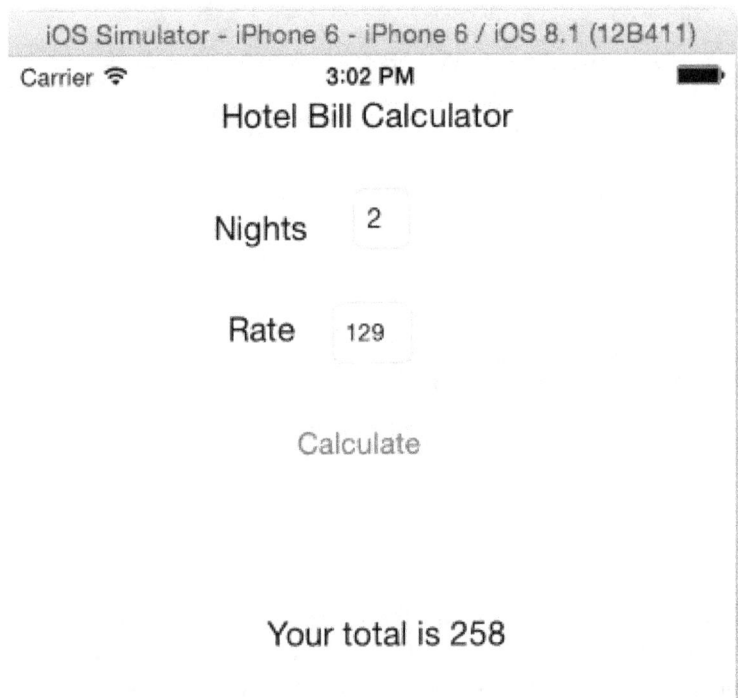

Coming from the Visual Basic world, I figured such an app would take at most 10 minutes to write. Alas, this was not the case. I learned that there are many, many differences between writing VB apps and writing iOS apps.

Contrasting Visual Studio and Xcode

To write an app like this in Visual Studio, you would create a new Windows Form application. You would drag labels for "Hotel Bill Calculator", "Nights", "Rate" and the "total message" onto the form, positioning them were you want. Next you'd drag on two text boxes to hold the values of the number of nights and the room rate. Finally, you would drag on a button.

To this point in the app, Xcode behaves virtually the same way. Xcode has labels, buttons, and input boxes. Cool! But at this point things begin to get *very* different.

In Visual Studio you click on a UI element to set its properties. One of the properties all UI elements are sure to have is a **Name** and once an element has a name you can refer to it in code by using the item's name.   If you have a button and you want to program what should happen when the button is clicked just click it in the editor and you will be taken to the appropriate code block. Not so in Xcode.

Outlets and Actions

Outlets

In Xcode if you want to refer to a UI element in code you first have to create something called an "outlet" for it. Once the outlet is created it works basically the same way but if you haven't created an outlet for the UI element the code cannot refer to it. Creating an outlet for a UI element in Xcode is the equivalent of giving it a name so you can refer to it in code.

Fortunately, creating an outlet isn't so hard once you get the hang of it-- and once you realize it is necessary.

Actions

The most common type of action in an application is a button push or a menu selection. In Visual Studio if you want to code what happens when a button is clicked, then you click it. This brings up a code window where you add the code that is associated with the button.

In Xcode if you want to code what happens when a button is clicked, you have to create an "action" for it.

We'll cover creating outlets and actions in the next section.

Lets Build an Application

For the rest of this chapter I'll walk you through building the hotel bill calculator application. In case you get stuck, the entire process is also available on youtube as a series of videos organized into a playlist.

If you are unable to click on the link above, just search youtube for **The Joy of Swift - Building your first iOS application**

To build the app, first start up Xcode and select File, New Project... You'll get a dialog box similar to the following:

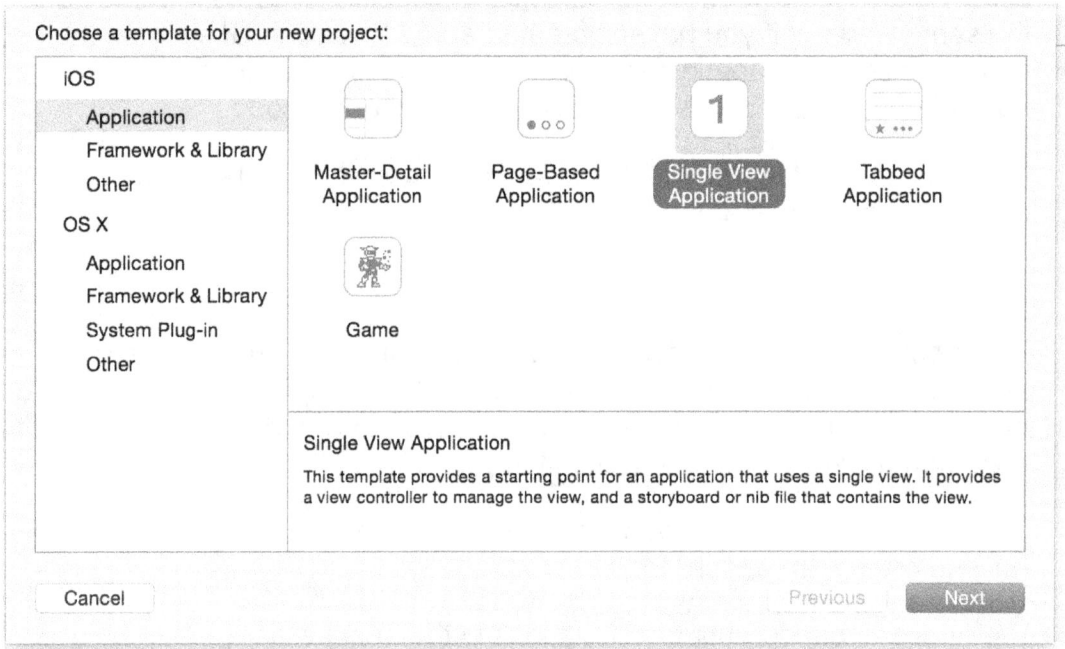

On the left side of the dialog box, be sure to select Application under the category of iOS. On the right side select **Single View Application**, then press Next.

Enter the product name, in this case "Hotel Bill Calculator". Also be sure the

Language is set to Swift and the Device is set to iPhone. Click Next.

The next dialog will ask you where to save the file. Just make a folder and put it in that. Finally, Xcode will go full screen.

Let's focus on the left side of the screen. The project navigator should be selected. If not, click on the thing I circled in the screen shot below:

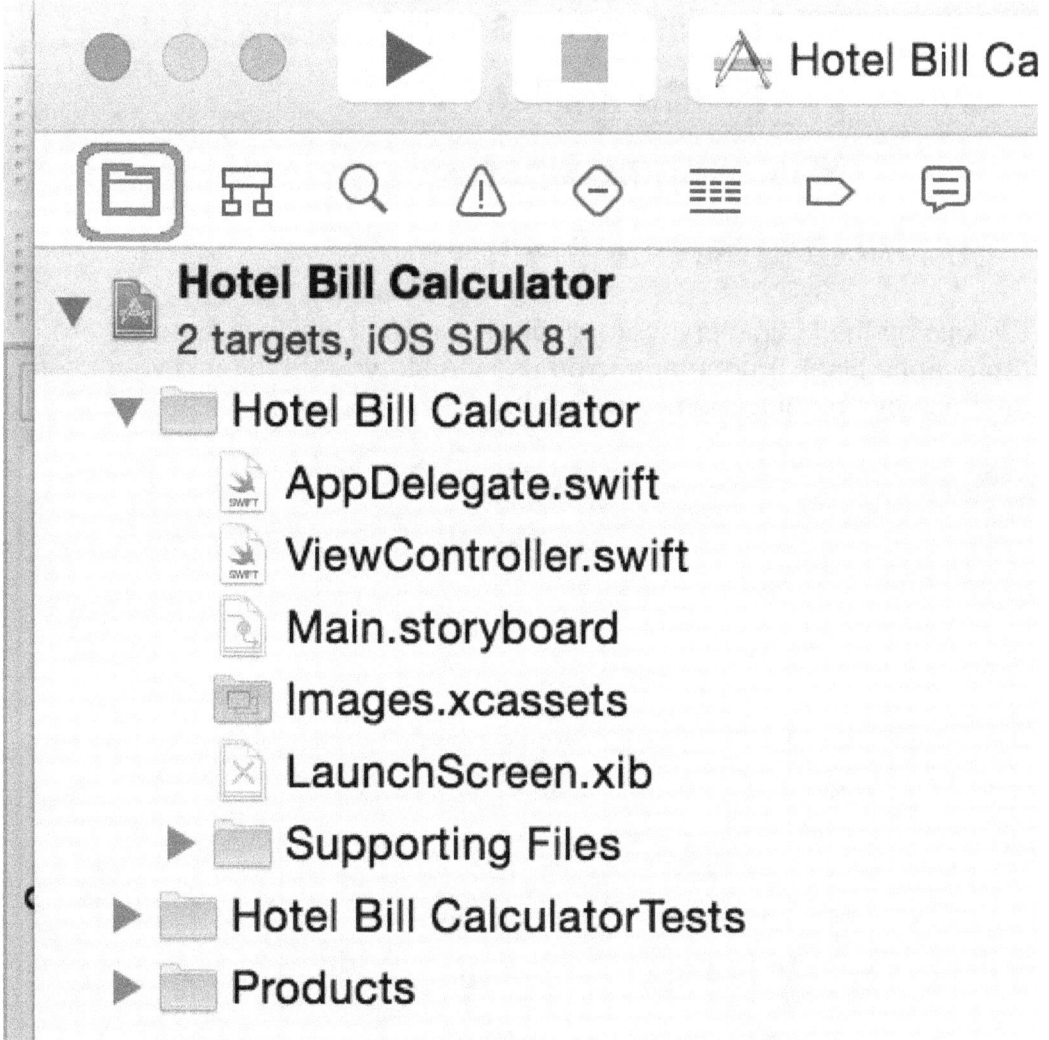

You'll notice a bunch of different items nested under the Hotel Bill Calculator folder. Click on the Main.storyboard, as shown:

Clicking on the Main.storyboard displays a screen which is supposed to represent a blank iPhone app. You use the storyboard to build your user interface by dragging elements onto it.

I clicked on the w**Any** /h**Any** indicator in the bottom center and set the device size to small for now. That keeps things simpler when getting started.

Hello World!

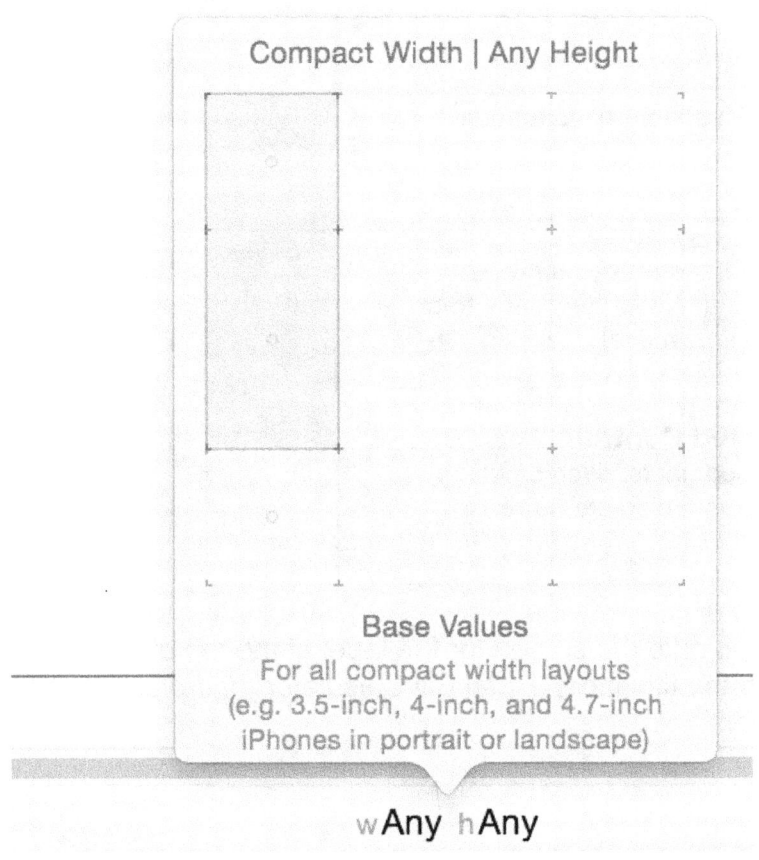

Building the User Interface

Labels

First let's add a couple of labels to the storyboard. In the bottom left corner of xCode you'll see a list of components. Scroll until you see label, the first item on the screenshot below:

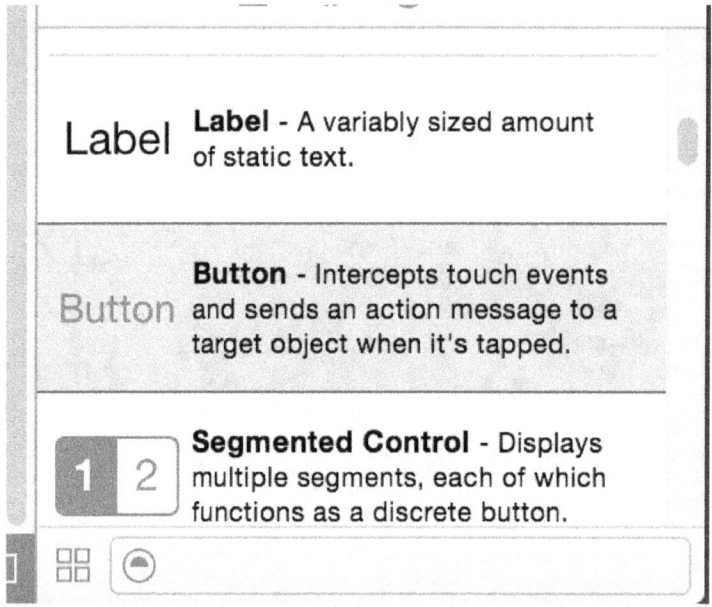

Select Label and drag it onto the screen for the label at the top of our application. Start with the title label "Hotel Bill Calculator" and drag it to the top center of the screen.

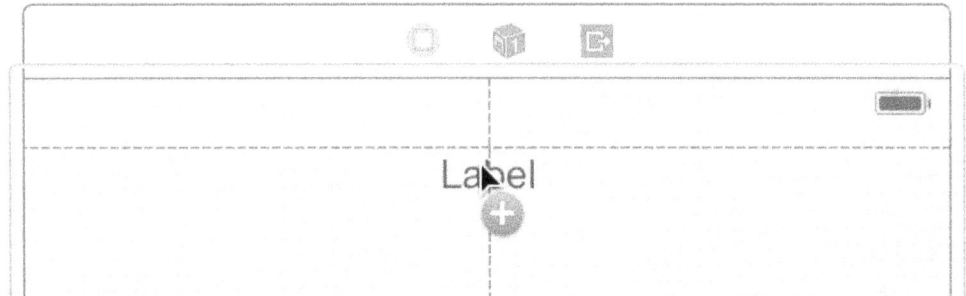

Click in the word Label and replace the text with "Hotel Bill Calculator". You may need to recenter it after that. Drag three more labels for Rate, Days, and Total.

Text Fields

Next we'll need a place for users to enter the appropriate values for the rate and days. Locate the control for text field and drag two onto the screen.

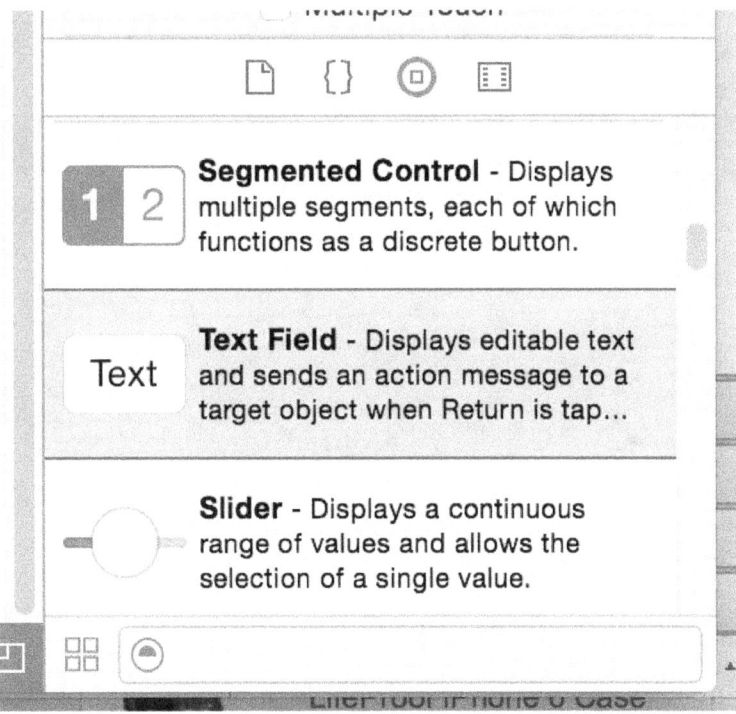

The two text boxes should be positioned next to their appropriate labels-- rate and days.   At this point you should have something like this:

Hotel Bill Calculator

Nights   2

Rate   129

Your total is 258

Adding Buttons

The next thing our application needs is a button that users can press so that their total will be calculated.

Drag the button onto the screen and change the text to read 'Calculate'. At this point you should have something like this:

Running your Program in the iOS Simulator

To run the application in the iOS simulator you first need to select the target device. For now select a 'small screen' device such as an iPhone 4 or 5. You can do this by clicking on the device name to the right of your project name in the top left corner of the Xcode window. In the screen shot below, I have selected iPhone 5s as the target device. If you see a different device in this spot, click on it and select the device you want.

If all goes well you'll see a "Build Succeeded" message similar to this:

Depending on the speed of your Mac the next thing that will appear is either the iOS simulator or an icon in the Dock letting you know that the simulator is loaded.   If you don't see the simulator right away, give it a moment. Once you see it in the dock you should be able to click on it and have your app appear:

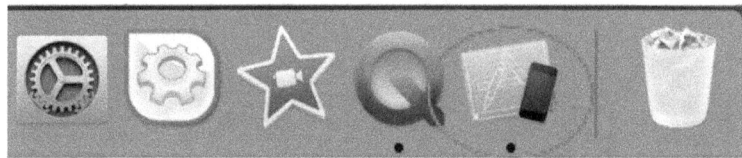

If the application doesn't look the way you expect, its probably because the Layout Constraints aren't done. Stop your program and select Add Missing Layout Constraints using the layout icon

Select Add Missing Constraints and run it again.

All Views in View Controller
Update Frames
Update Constraints
Add Missing Constraints
Reset to Suggested Constraints
Clear Constraints

Link the Storyboard to Code

Next we are going to create some code to allow the hotel bill calculator to function. For this part you have to be able to click and drag from the storyboard into the code window so **both** windows need to be visible.

If you have an icon in your toolbar that looks like a two rings, you can click that icon to toggle this setting on and off.

If you don't have the two rings icon then you may have an earlier of Xcode which used a different icon that looked like a tuxedo.

If you don't have that icon either then there is an alternate way to get the screen arranged as required and that is to select **View, Assistant Editor, Show Assistant Editor**, as shown below:

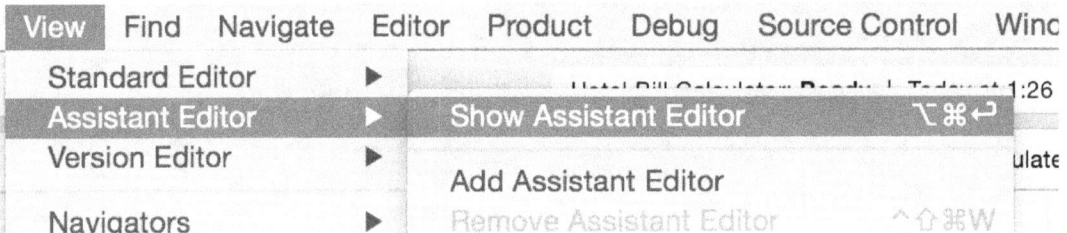

The Assistant button splits the Xcode editor in two, with your primary work document on the left and an intelligent Assistant editor pane to the right.

We want to be able to access our text fields from code and to do that you need to create an 'Outlet'. Select an element on the screen such as the text box next to the Rate label then press and hold the control key. Then drag your mouse to the code window as shown:

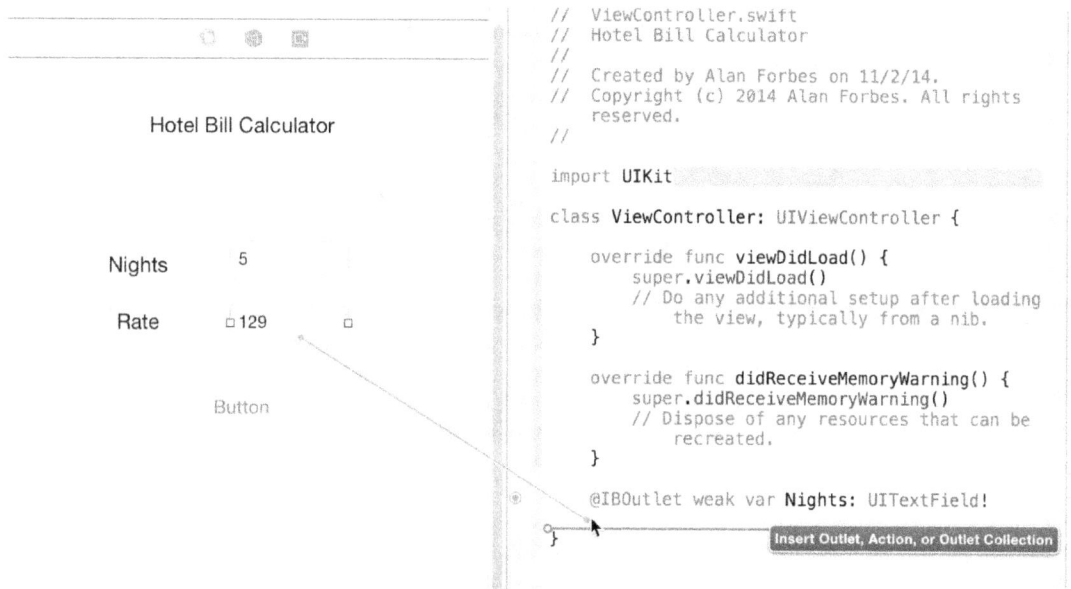

```
// ViewController.swift
// Hotel Bill Calculator
//
// Created by Alan Forbes on 11/2/14.
// Copyright (c) 2014 Alan Forbes. All rights
     reserved.
//

import UIKit

class ViewController: UIViewController {

    override func viewDidLoad() {
        super.viewDidLoad()
        // Do any additional setup after loading
            the view, typically from a nib.
    }

    override func didReceiveMemoryWarning() {
        super.didReceiveMemoryWarning()
        // Dispose of any resources that can be
            recreated.
    }

    @IBOutlet weak var Nights: UITextField!

}
```

When you let go you should see a pop-up window that will allow you to insert an outlet or an action as shown below:

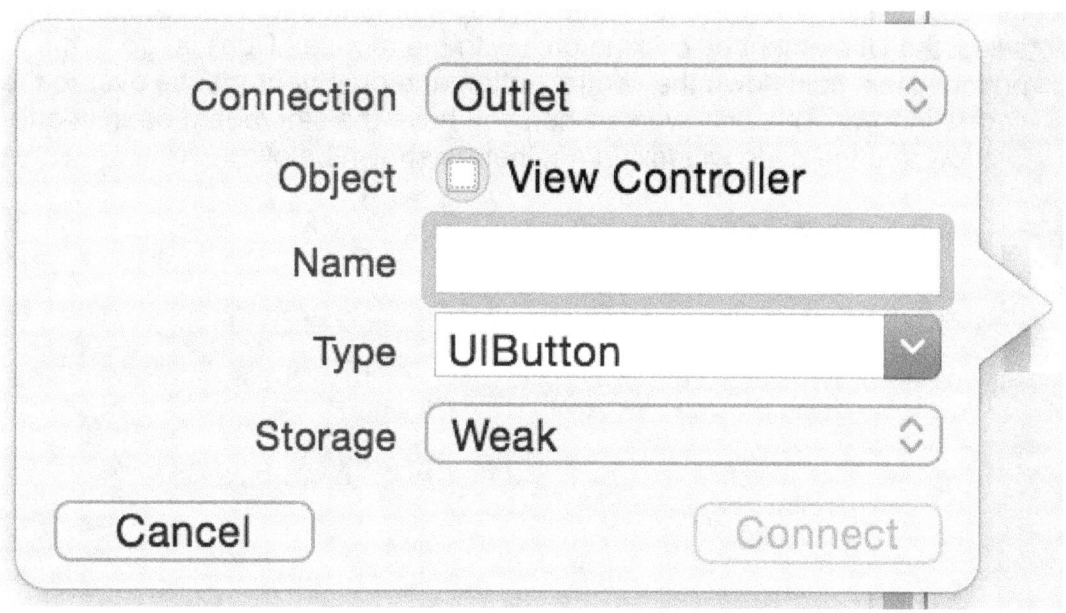

To the right of the word connection, be sure to select Outlet. Give the item a meaningful name, such as Rate. Xcode will create some code similar to:

`@IBOutlet weak var Rate: UITextField!`

Congratulations, you have created your first outlet and we can now refer to this text box in code.

Do the same thing for the other text box and also for the Bill Total label. When you are done you should have code similar to:

`@IBOutlet weak var Nights: UITextField!`

`@IBOutlet weak var Rate: UITextField!`

`@IBOutlet weak var Total: UILabel!`

Creating Outlets and Actions

In Xcode, when you want to create an outlet or action for a particular item you select the UI element by clicking on it with the mouse. Don't let go of the button. Next hold down the control button and drag your mouse over to the code window.   This only works when you have the storyboard open in one window and the code window in another as shown below:

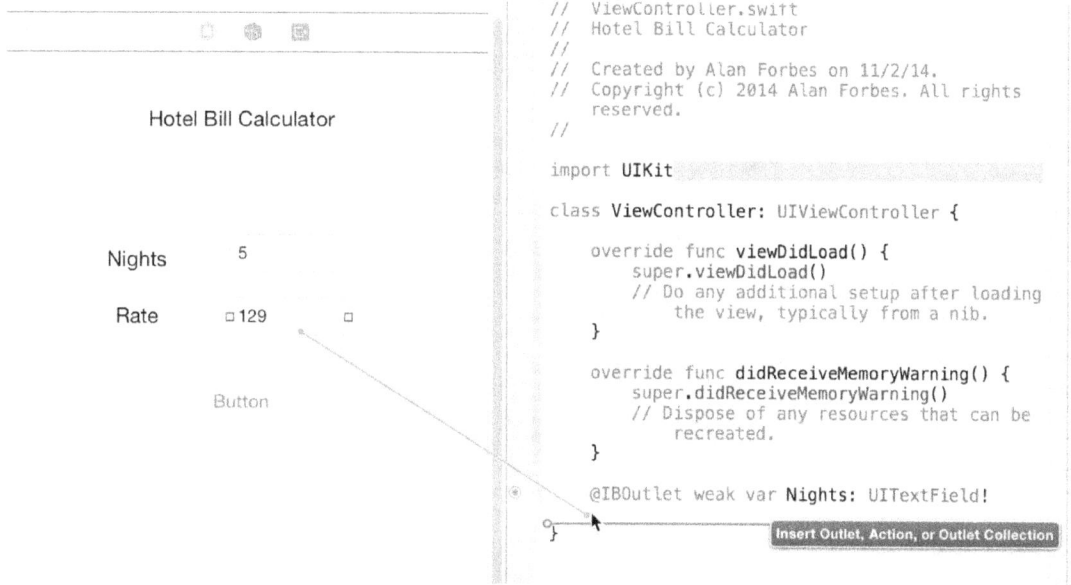

As you begin dragging your mouse to the code window, you'll see that it makes a line that stretches from the control to your mouse. Drag it all the way to the code window and release the mouse.

At this point Xcode will ask you if you want to create an outlet, action, or outlet collection by displaying the following dialog box:

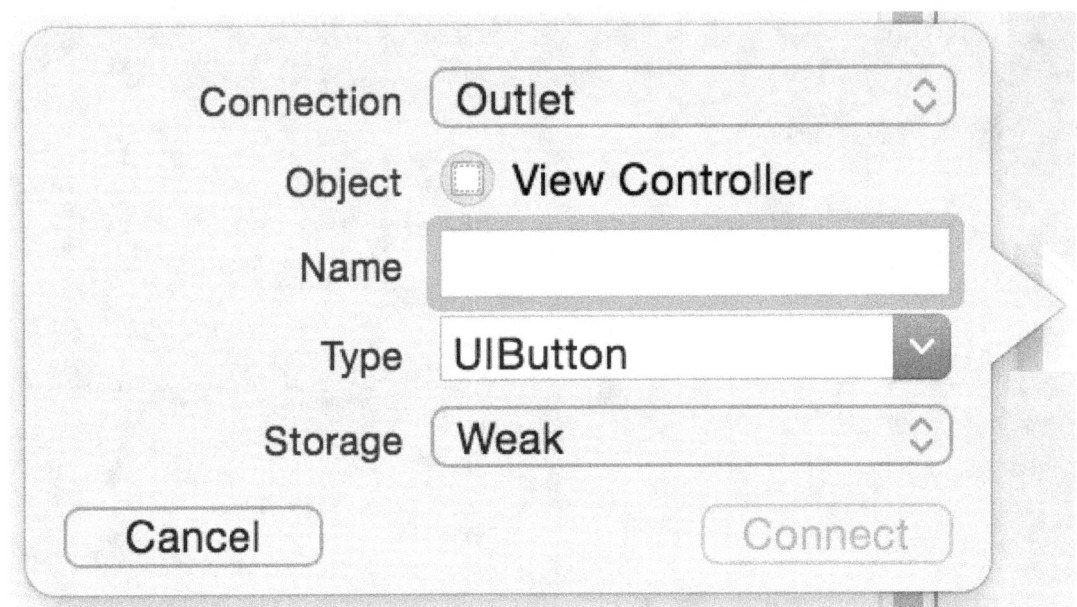

The top box that says Outlet in the screen shot can be clicked on to change from outlet to action. The highlighted field (Name) is where you provide a name for the element. Then you can use this name later in your code.

For example, in the Hotel Bill Calculator application we need to read the values entered by the user into the Nights box and the Rate box and multiply those numbers together and write the result into the total bill label. If you drag an outlet into the code window for the rate box and provide a name, Xcode will add code to the code window that then allows you to refer to the element in code.

The code that was added is:

```
@IBOutlet weak var Nights: UITextField!
```

The part of the code that matters to us is that a new var named **Nights** was created and it refers to an object of type UITextField.

```
                                          @IBAction func TestButton(sender:
                                             AnyObject) {
                                          }
```

In the screen shot above I am highlighting the filled circle to the right of the code. When you do this Xcode will highlight the item that the code is linked to. The gray line connecting the two elements is not part of Xcode. I added the line for clarity.

Follow the same technique to create an action for a button, but be sure to change the selector from action to outlet when you let go of the mouse. In the case of an action, Xcode will create slightly different code:

The code created by Xcode is

@IBAction func TestButton(sender: AnyObject) {

    }

It creates a new function called **TestButton** (the name I gave it) which is linked to the button we dragged from. The thing to note is that the code snippet includes the curly braces { }. Inside the curly braces is where you put the code you want executed when the button is clicked.

Making the Calculate Button Work

Getting back to our Hotel Bill Calculator application follow the procedure outlined above to create an Action for the Calculate button.

Initially you'll see something like this:

@IBAction func btnCalculate(sender: AnyObject) {

}

Typically the first thing you want to do is just make sure the connection works before you do any coding. So the first bit of code you might add is a simple print line statement to see if you get the message when the button is pushed.   Add the following bit of code then run the project.

```
@IBAction func btnCalculate(sender: AnyObject) {

    print("The button was pushed")

}
```

When you run the application and press the button, you should see your message in what's called the debug window. It will look like this:

Button Pushed

To make the code actually calculate the user's total hotel bill will take a bit more code. I've numbered the code below and will walk you through it.

```
1.      @IBAction func btnCalculate(sender: AnyObject) {
2.          print("The button was pushed")
3.          if let numNights = Nights.text.toInt(){
4.              if let myRate = Rate.text.toInt()
5.              {
6.                  var myTotal = numNights * myRate
7.                  print(myTotal)
8.                  Total.text = "Your total is \(myTotal)"
9.              }
10.         }
11.     }
```

Line 1 is the action we created by dragging the button to the code window. By the way, it's called an IBAction rather than an Action because we created it using the Interface Builder (IB). **Line 1** ends with an open curly brace { indicating the start of the code block. These braces always have to be closed and this particular brace is closed on **line 12**.

Line 2 is the line we added to get a message to print to the debug window. It does not contribute to the calculation.

Before we can multiply the two numbers together you need to check that the user *actually entered* numbers. If we were **sure** that the user entered a number in the number of nights box, we could convert it into an integer using the toInt() function as so:

```
let numNights = Nights.text.toInt()
```

But since you never quite know what users will do, **Line 3** actually wraps the above statement in an if statement to test whether Nights.text (the text value in the box) can be converted into an integer.

```
if let numNights = Nights.text.toInt(){
```

If we can assign the variable numNights an integer value we execute the code block that follows in the curly brackets. This is why **Line 2** ends with {. This block is closed on **Line 10**.

Line 4 performs the same test on the Rate field. If it can be converted to an integer yet another code block is executed inside a pair of curly braces-- lines 6, 7, and 8. This is the code that calculates the total. These lines are repeated below as **lines 1 – 3** so you don't have to scroll back up to the original code block.

```
1.          var myTotal = numNights * myRate
2.          print(myTotal)
3.          Total.text = "Your total is \(myTotal)"
```

Line 1 declares a variable called myTotal and sets its value to the product of numNights and myRate.

Line 2 prints the total to the debug window to make it easier for the programmer (you) to follow along.

Line 3 updates the text value of the Total label with a new string. We could only update the Total label because we created an outlet for it.

15

Working with Images

Introduction

Images can make an application look more interesting and professional looking, when used appropriately. Contrast these two applications. Which would you rather use?

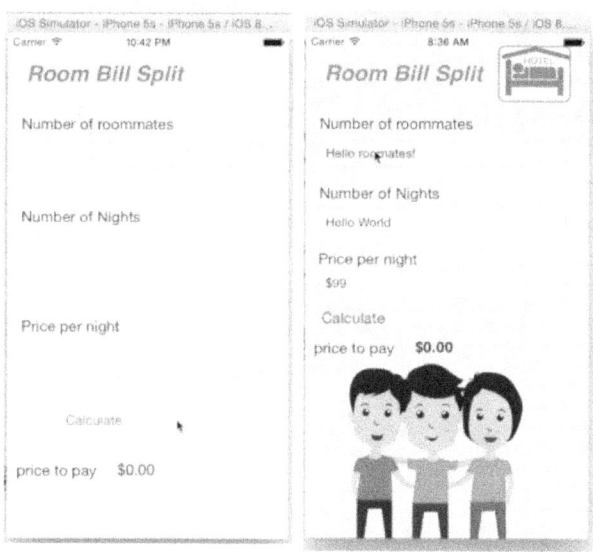

It doesn't matter if you can see the images perfectly or not, the question is which one catches *your* eye?

Adding Images to your Project File

Before you can use images in your application, you must first add those images to your project file.   Fortunately, this is pretty easy to do.

First put all the images you need in a folder. Then drag this folder from a Finder window onto your Xcode project. Drag it onto the folder in which you find your Main storyboard, as shown in the screen shot below:

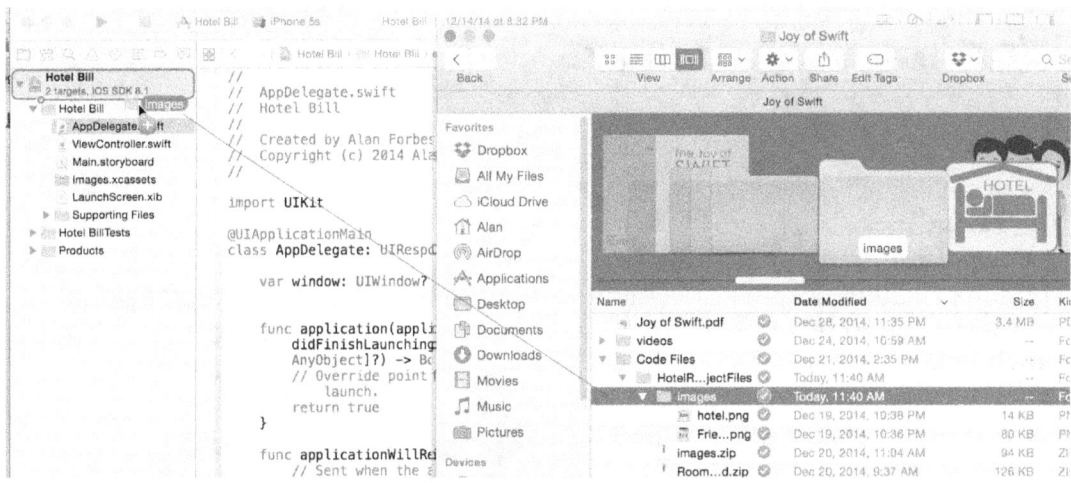

Once you have dragged the files into your project, Xcode will present you with an options box. I recommend you select Copy Items if needed and Create groups, as shown

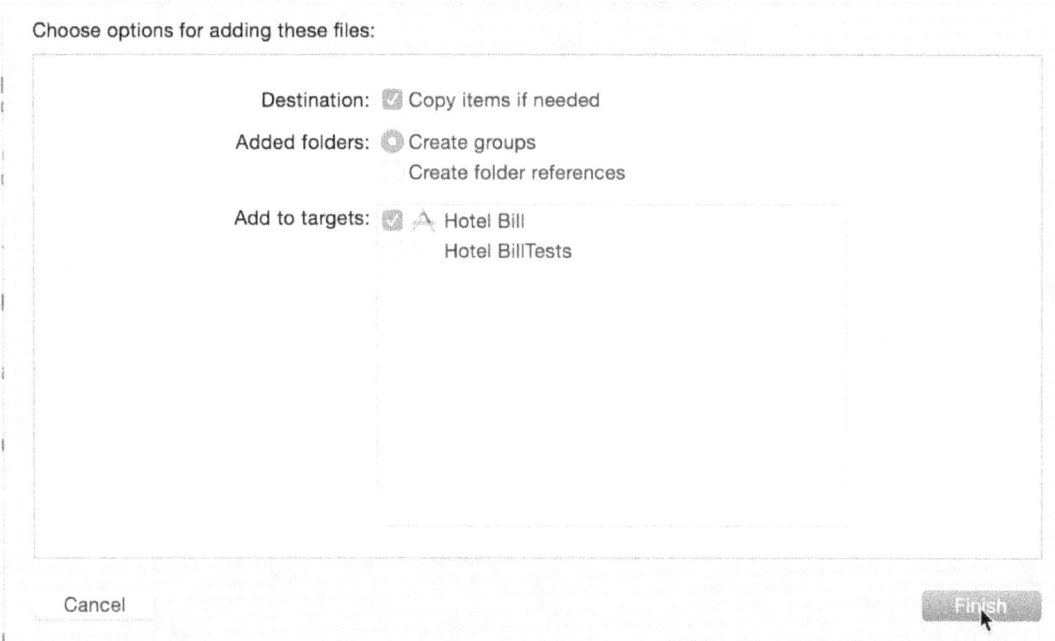

Choose options for adding these files:

Destination: ☑ Copy items if needed

Added folders: ○ Create groups
Create folder references

Add to targets: ☑ 𝖠 Hotel Bill
Hotel BillTests

Cancel   Finish

Now you'll be able to reference these images in your project.

Using the Image Control

With images imported into your project you can then use the image control to place the images onto your storyboard.

Locate the collection of controls that is in the left corner of the Xcode window and either scroll until you locate the Image View or simply search for as described in the next section:

Search Available Controls

If you know what you're looking for, you can also type any part of the word that matches the desired control (in this case, 'image') into the search bar and Xcode will locate the control for you. In the screen shot below, I typed the circled word.

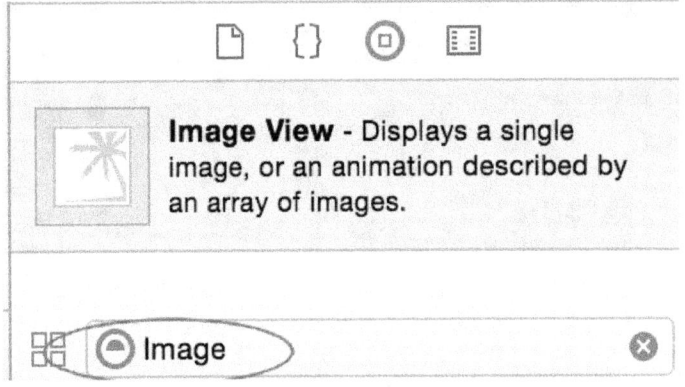

Image View - Displays a single image, or an animation described by an array of images.

Image

Adding an Image to your Application

Drag the Image View control onto your storyboard and place it where you want it and size it appropriately.

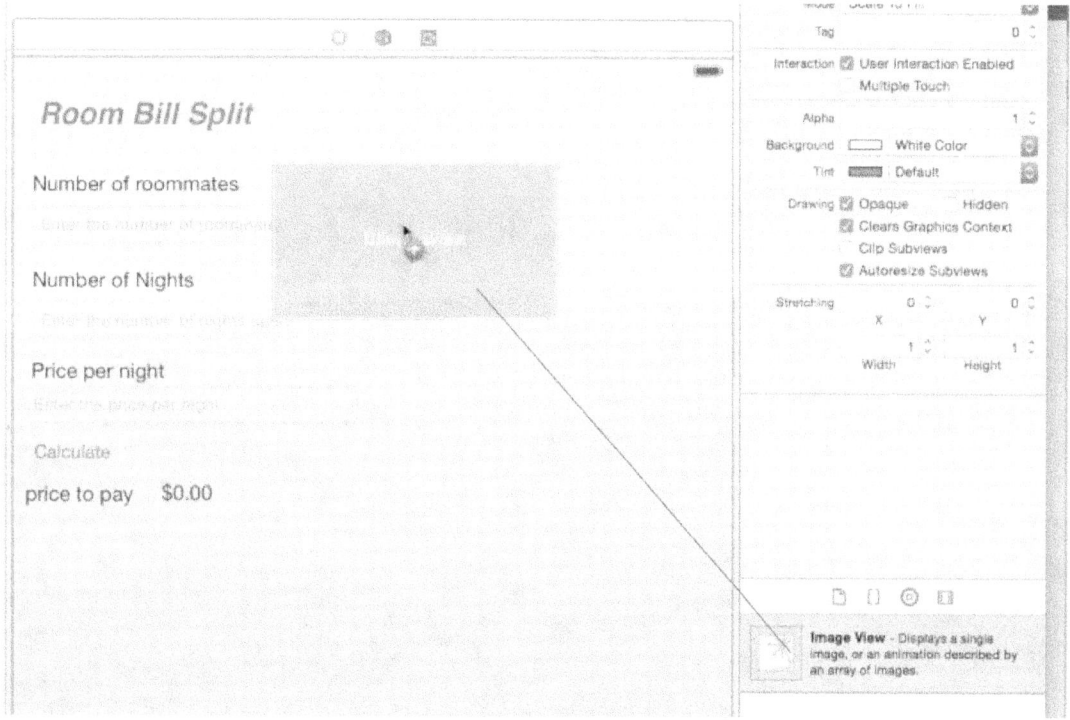

Next you click on the image attributes and start typing the name of one of the images you added to the project. At some point Xcode will fill in the possible matches and you can just select that.

Once the Image View control has an image associated with it the image will be drawn in the rectangle and you can see exactly how it will look.

16

Working with the iOS UI Controls

Introduction

Xcode comes with a variety of controls that you can use in your project. A control is a way to allow your app to communicate with a user. Controls convey a particular action or intention to the app through user interaction, and can be used to manipulate content, provide user input, navigate within an app, or execute other actions which you, as the developer, can define.

The controls available in Xcode are simple to use and familiar to users because the appear throughout many iOS apps. The `UIControl` class is the base class for all controls on iOS and defines the functionality common to all controls.   By using controls carefully and consistently in your app you can convey to users the intention of the app and allow them to figure out how to use it.

Typical Controls

Here are some typical iOS controls:

- Buttons
- Date Pickers
- Page Controls

- Segmented Controls
- Text Fields
- Sliders
- Steppers
- Switches

In the next few chapters I'll talk about each of these controls and how to use them with Swift. Each control will have its own project to keep things simple. Of course, in a real-world project you would likely combine several controls onto a single page in an app.

Create a Basic Project

For each of the following chapters we'll start off with a base project. Rather than repeat these steps each time, I'll describe how to create a basic project here once and subsequent chapters will refer to it.

Open Xcode and create a new single view Application. For product name, use the name of the control that we are learning and fill out the rest of the form with your usual values. Enter **Swift** as language and select **iPhone** in devices.

Go to the Storyboard. Since these sample apps are only going to be for the iPhone, you can disable size classes. In the File Inspector deselect Use Size Classes. You'll find that option in the group box titled **Interface Builder Document**, as shown below:

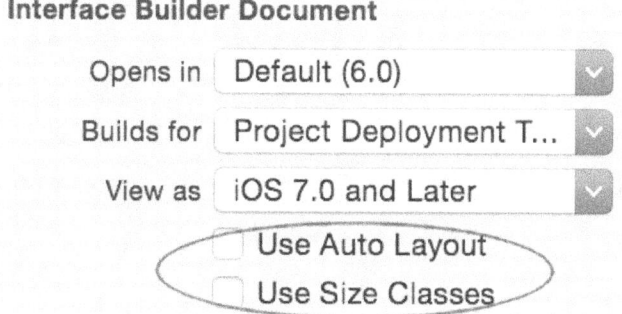

When prompted, select Keep size class data for: iPhone. Whenever you need a new project as you follow along in subsequent chapters simply create a new project following this basic outline.

17

Working with the UISlider

Introduction

A Slider is a visual control used to select a single value from a continuous range of values. Sliders are typically displayed as horizontal bars. An indicator is used to display the current value of the slider and it can be moved by the user to change the value.

In this tutorial, we display an UISlider and a Label. When the user moves the slider, the numeric value of the slider will be displayed in the Label.

Create a Slider Project

Create a basic project as described in the previous chapter and name it Slider Control.

Add UI Elements

Drag a Slider to the main view and span its width to the width of the main View. Select the slider and go to the Attributes inspector. Under the slider section change the maximum value to 100 and change the current value to 0.

The thumb of the slider will move to the left side indicating the current value of 0, which you just set.

Next, drag a label to the main view and position it below the slider. Center the text and change it to 0.

The Storyboard should look similar to this.

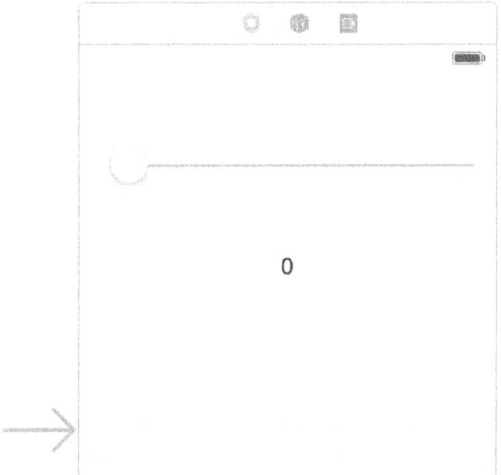

Next, either click on the button in the bottom right corner of the storyboard that says "Resolve Auto Layout Issues" (circled in the image below) or manually set the layout constraints by control-dragging from the edges of the control to the the edges of the storyboard. You have to do this to get the controls to look right when you run it in the simulator and on actual devices.

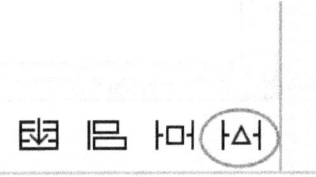

Add Outlets and Actions

Select the Assistant Editor and make sure the ViewController.swift file is visible. Press and hold the control key and drag from the Slider to the ViewController class to create an outlet.

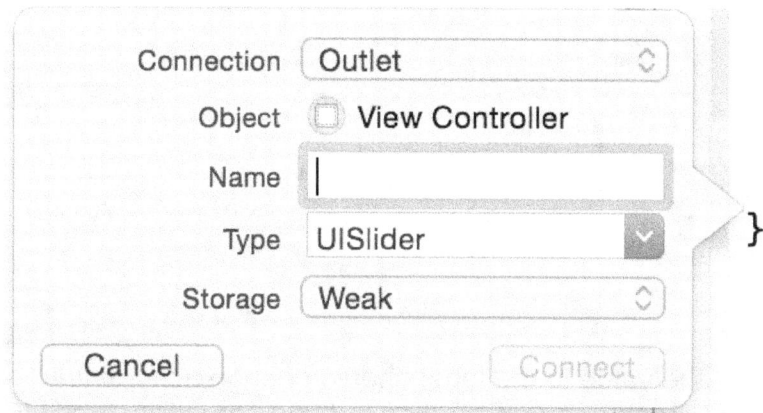

Connection	Outlet	
Object	☐ View Controller	
Name		
Type	UISlider	▾
Storage	Weak	
Cancel		Connect

Next, press and hold the control key and drag from the Label to the Viewcontroller class and create another outlet.

Finally, Ctrl and Drag from the Slider to the ViewController class and create an action for the slider.

Code the Action

Go to the ViewController.swift file and add the following code to the sliderValueChanged Action method

```
@IBAction func sliderValueChanged(sender: UISlider) {
  var currentValue = Int(sender.value)
  label.text = "\(currentValue)"
}
```

The slider's sender.value is of type float so we convert it to an integer using the Int function built into Swift.

Build and Run the project and move the slider to the middle of the bar.

Your new app should look similar to this:

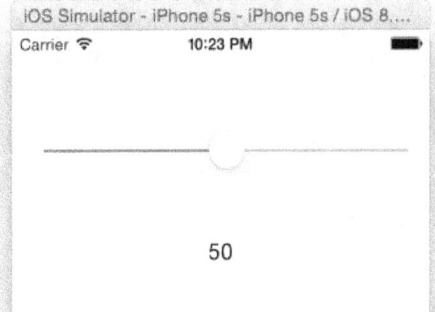

As you move the slider, the value in the label should change accordingly. You may think this is not much of an application but you are learning building blocks that you can apply into your own applications. For example, later in this book we'll make an application that plays sounds such as mp3 files and we'll use the slider control to allow the user to set the volume.

18

Working with the UIDatePicker

Introduction

The Date Picker component (UIDatePicker) uses multiple rotating wheels to allow users to select dates and times. In this chapter we'll read the value selected by the user and present it in a label.

 When the user moves the date picker, the date and time values of the control will be displayed in the label.

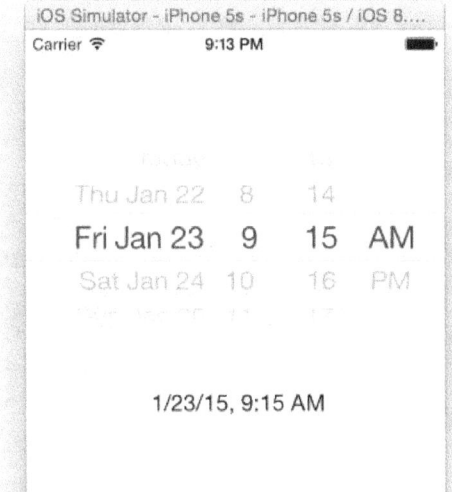

Create a Date Picker Project

Create a basic project as described in the previous chapter and name it Date Picker. Go to the Storyboard.

Add the UI Elements

Drag a UIDatePicker control and an label control onto the storyboard. The date picker will take up the entire width of the screen. Extend the label so that it also extends across the width of the screen and select center alignment.

Double click on the label to exit the existing text and enter some date format such as MM/DD/YY, HH:MM so that you will know what is supposed to go into that place later. Your storyboard should now look like this:

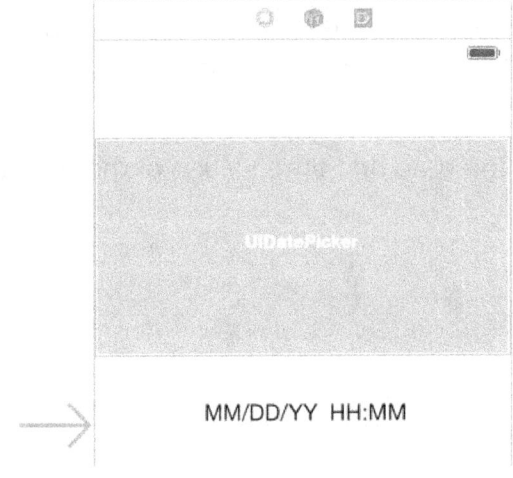

Next, either click on the button in the bottom right corner of the storyboard that says "Resolve Auto Layout Issues" (circled in the image below) or manually set the layout constraints by control-dragging from the edges of the control to the the edges of the storyboard. You have to do this to get the controls to look right when you run it in the simulator and on actual devices.

Add Outlets and Actions

Click the icon that looks like two blue circles to show the Assistant Editor. Select the UIDatePicker. Press and hold the control key and drag to the code window. You should be prompted to create an Outlet or Action. Create an outlet and call it datePicker. In the screen shot below I capitalize the D but you should know that the Apple coding convention is that the first letter should be lower case, so this is a stylistic mistake. **datePicker** would be a better name.

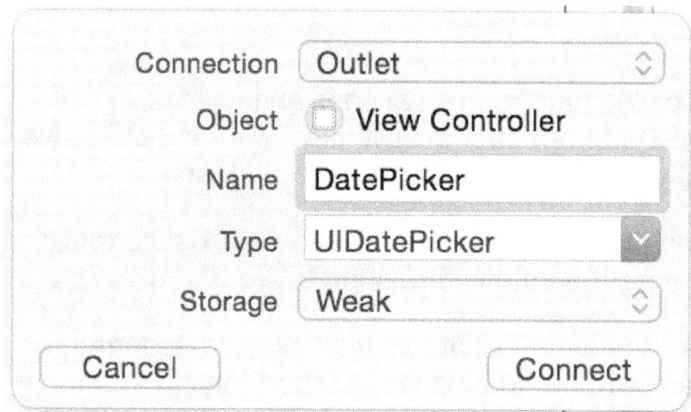

Repeat this step to create an Outlet for the label too. Now our code can talk to the UI components.

Next we need to create an Action for the date picker. When the user changes the date by clicking one of the wheels, we want the label to be updated with the date selected.

Select the UIDatePicker. Press and hold the control key and drag to the code window. You should be prompted to create an Outlet or Action. Create an Action and call it datePickerChanged.

Code the Action

Next we need to code what happens when the date picker changes. Find the code that was created when we created the UIDatePicker Action, which should look like this:

```
@IBAction func datePickerChanged(sender: AnyObject) {
}
```

Add the following code inside the empty code block:

```
1.    var dateFormat = NSDateFormatter()
2.    dateFormat.dateStyle = NSDateFormatterStyle.ShortStyle
3.    dateFormat.timeStyle = NSDateFormatterStyle.ShortStyle
4.    var strDate = dateFormat.stringFromDate(datePicker.date)
5.    dateLabel.text = strDate
```

Line 1 creates a variable called dateFormat which is an instance of the NSDateFormatter. The NSDateFormatter is built into Swift (and Objective C) and is used to convert native date objects into formatted strings.

Line 2 tells Swift that when the dateFormat variable is called to format a specific date, it should provide the date in the "short" style.

Line 3 tells Swift that when the dateFormat variable is called to format a specific date, it should also provide the time in the "short" style.

Line 4 creates new string variable called strDate. The value of the variable strDate comes from the dateFormat variable, which in turn is provided a date to format using the stringFromDate method. The stringFromDate method is passed the current value of the datePicker.

Finally, **Line 5** sets the text of the UILabel to the value of the strDate variable, which is a formatted string which includes the short version of the date and the short version of the time.

Your final code block should look like this:

```
@IBAction func datePickerChanged(sender: AnyObject) {
    var dateFormat = NSDateFormatter()
    dateFormat.dateStyle = NSDateFormatterStyle.ShortStyle
    dateFormat.timeStyle = NSDateFormatterStyle.ShortStyle
    var strDate = dateFormat.stringFromDate(datePicker.date)
    dateLabel.text = strDate
}
```

On Your Own

See if you can experiment with the application to get different text displayed in the box. For instance, just the date or just the time. How about getting the UIDatePicker to only display the date?

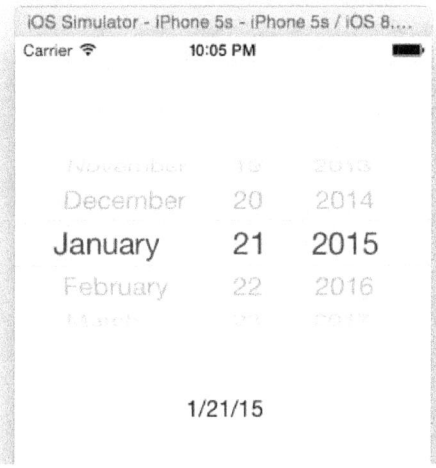

19

Working with the Segmented Control

Introduction

The segmented control is made up of a number of individual buttons called segments. When the user presses one of the buttons, it stays lit up until another button is pressed. In this chapter we'll read the value selected by the user and present it in a label.

Create a Segmented Control Project

Create a basic project as described in the previous chapter and name it Segmented Control. Go to the Storyboard.

Add the UI Elements

Drag a Segmented control and a label control onto the storyboard. When you first create it the control will have two segments. In our project we want three segments. Select the control then look to the right corner of Xcode for a control panel similar to the one below. Find the box labeled Segments and change the number from 2 to 3:

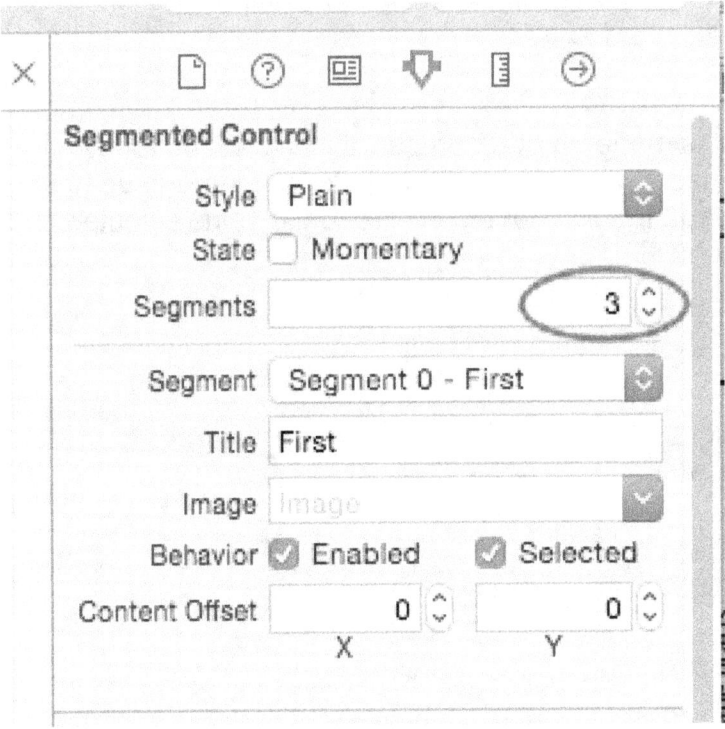

Next we need to give the third segment a label. Click the spinner control labeled **Segment** (which will have the value **Segment 0 – First** in it. Click the drop down and select segment 2. It might seem strange to you that the **third** segment is segment **2**, but it make sense when you realize that the first element is zero and the second one is one. Thus, the third segment is two. If you're new to programming you'll come across this many times. It is consistent with the idea of an array, with the first element starting at zero.

Once you have selected **Segment 2**, the Title box will be empty:

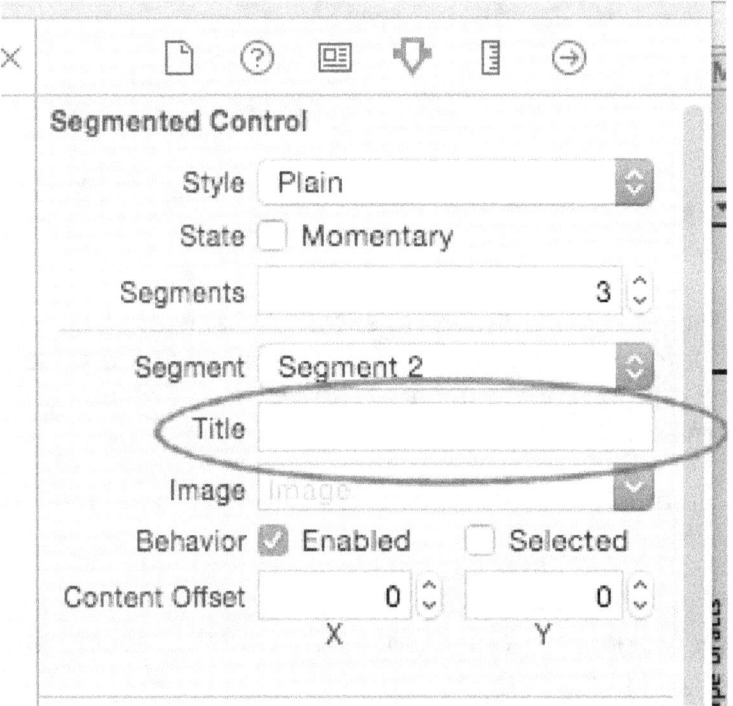

Enter the text "Third Segment" into the title field.

Extend the label so that it also extends across the width of the screen and select center alignment. Then, as we've seen before you need to add layout constraints so it will look right across different devices.

Double click on the label to exit the existing text and enter some text such as **Select a Segment** so that you will know where the text box when you run your application. Your storyboard should now look like this:

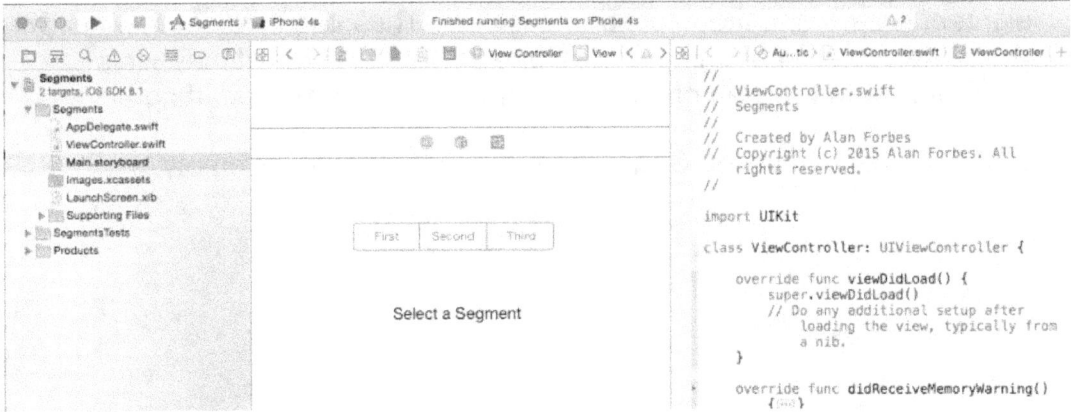

Add Outlets and Actions

Click the icon that looks like two blue circles to show the Assistant Editor. Select the segmented control. Press and hold the control key and drag to the code window. You should be prompted to create an Outlet or Action. Create an outlet and call it **segmentControl**.

Repeat this step to create an Outlet for the label too. Now our code can talk to the UI components.

Next we need to create an Action for the segmented control. When the user changes the selection by clicking one of the items, we want the label to be updated based on the segment selected.

Select the segment control. Press and hold the control key and drag to the code window. You should be prompted to create an Outlet or Action. Create an Action and call it **segmentChanged**.

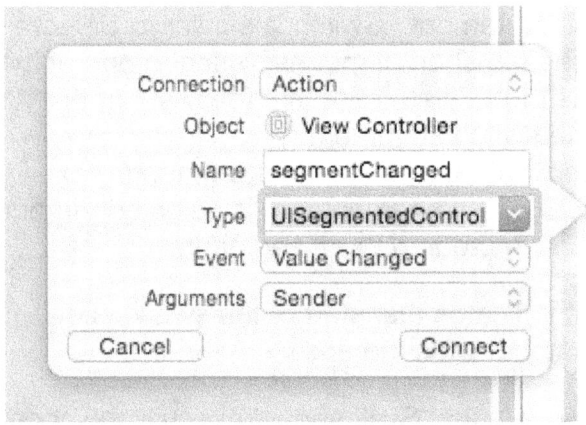

The Type field defaults to AnyObject but we want to change to type UISegmentedControl, as shown above.

Code the Action

Next we need to code what happens when the user clicks on the segment control causing the selected segment to change. Find the code that was created when we created the segmentChanged Action, which should look like this:

```
@IBAction func segmentChanged(sender: UISegmentedControl) {}
```

Add the following code inside the empty code block:

```
1.      switch segmentControl.selectedSegmentIndex
2.          {
3.          case 0:
4.              label.text = "First Segment";
5.          case 1:
6.              label.text = "Second Segment";
7.          case 2:
8.              label.text = "Third Segment";
9.          default:
10.             break;
11.         }
```

Line 1 is the beginning of a switch statement. Switch is similar to Select Case statements in other languages. In short, it means switch to one of the following cases based on the value of the statement that follows. In this case, the statement that follows the switch statement is **segmentControl.selectedSegmentIndex.** The selectedSegmentIndex of the segmentControl is the index number of the segment that is selected. In our case it will either be 0, 1, or 2 since we created three segments.

Line 2 is the open curly brace that indicates that start of the switch code. **Line 11** is the close curly brace that indicates the end.

Line 3 says **case 0:** What this means is that Swift should execute the code that follows if the selectedSegmentIndex of the segmentControl is zero. In other words, if the the first segment is clicked we will set the text of the label control to read "First Segment". This happens in **Line 4**.

Lines 5 -8 handle the cases of the other two segments being selected.

Finally, **Line 9** handles the case of what to do if any other value is returned by the segmented control. You might think to yourself that there is no way that this function will get any value other than 0, 1, or 2 and you'll be right! But what if someone changes the segmented control later and doesn't update the function properly. In that case you'd get a crash. So it is a best practice to always include a default: block in a switch statement.

Your final code to run this entire project should look like this:

```
@IBOutlet weak var label: UILabel!
@IBOutlet weak var segmentControl: UISegmentedControl!

@IBAction func segmentChanged(sender: UISegmentedControl) {

    switch segmentControl.selectedSegmentIndex
    {
    case 0:
        label.text = "First Segment";
    case 1:
        label.text = "Second Segment";
```

```
    case 2:
      label.text = "Third Segment";
    default:
      break;
    }
}
```

On Your Own

Exercise 1:

You may notice that when the application first starts the first segment is selected but the text says 'Select a Segment'. You can't actually get the app to display First Segment without first selecting another segment.

How can you make this better?

Exercise 2:

A switch is a control that has two states – on and off. Can you figure out how to apply the lessons from this chapter to display "Switch is On" and "Switch is Off" based on the value of a switch control?

20

Working with the UIWebView Control

Introduction

The **UIWebView** control is a browser control that you can program.   In this basic example, the UIWebView control will navigate to the URL specified in the text box when the user presses the Go button.

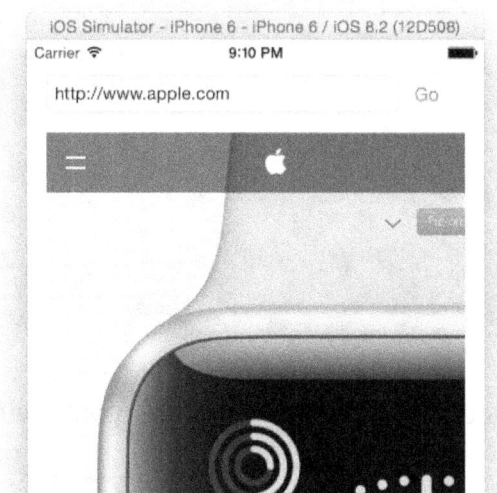

Create a WebUIView Control Project

Create a basic project as described in a previous chapter and name it WebView. Go to the Storyboard.

Add the UI Elements

Drag a text field and an button control onto the storyboard and arrange at the top of the screen. Next drag a WebUIView control onto the screen and arrange it to fill the remaining screen real estate, as shown below:

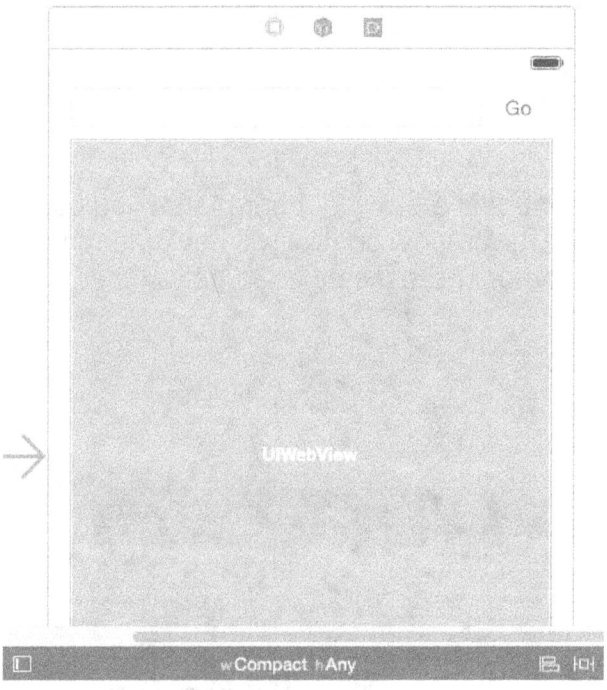

Then, as we've seen before you need to add layout constraints so it will look right across different devices.

Add Outlets and Actions

Click the icon that looks like two blue circles to show the Assistant Editor.

Select the UITextControl control. Press and hold the control key and drag to the code window. You should be prompted to create an Outlet or Action. Create an outlet and call it **txtURL**.

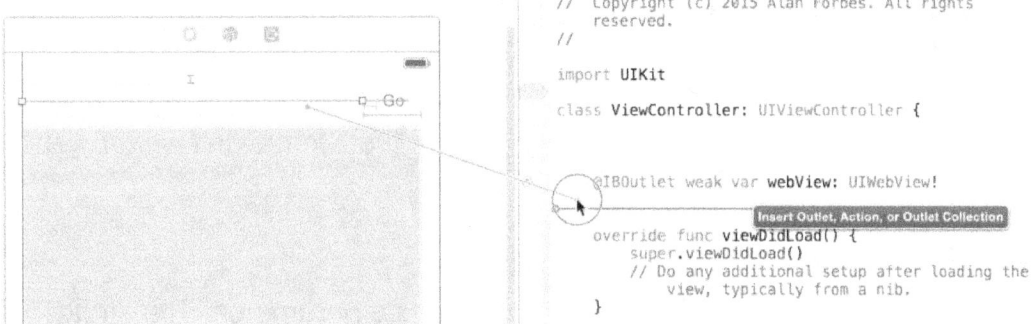

Repeat this step to create an Outlet for the UIWebControl too. Now our code can talk to the UI components.

Next we need to create an Action for the button control. When the user clicks the button, we want the UIWebControl to be updated based on the text entered in the text box.

Select the button control. Press and hold the control key and drag to the code window. You should be prompted to create an Outlet or Action. Create an Action and call it **pushedGo**.

Code the Action

Next we need to code what happens when the user clicks on the segment control causing the selected segment to change. Find the code that was created when we created the segmentChanged Action, which should look like this:

@IBAction func pushedGo(sender: UIButton) {}

Add the following code inside the empty code block:

loadAddressURL(txtURL.text)

The code block in its entirety will look like this:

```
@IBAction func pushedGo(sender: UIButton) {
    loadAddressURL(txtURL.text)
}
```

The line loadAddressURL is calling a function that we haven't written yet.

The loadAddressURL Function

We will write a function which takes a string as a parameter. The string parameter will tell the functional which URL to load into the UIWebView control.

Write the following code:

```
1.      func loadAddressURL(URLPath: String){
2.          let requestURL = NSURL(string:URLPath)
3.          let request = NSURLRequest(URL: requestURL!)
4.          webView.loadRequest(request)
5.      }
```

Line 1 declares the function as having the name of **loadAddressURL** which takes one parameter – (URLPath: String). This format is in two parts; the first part is the name of the variable we can use to access the parameter in our function, and the second part specifies what type to expect. In this case, we expect to get a string.

Line 2 declares a variable called **requestURL** which is set as an NSURL object, which is built into iOS and OSX. When you create an NSURL object you have to pass it a string in URL format.

An `NSURL` object represents a URL that can potentially contain the location of a resource on a remote server, the path of a local file on disk, or even an arbitrary piece of encoded data.

Line 3 declares a variable called **request** an which is set as an NSURLRequest object, which is also built into iOS and OSX.

```
let request = NSURLRequest(URL: requestURL!)
```

When you create an NSURLRequest object you have to pass it an NSURL object, which we created in **line 2.**

> `NSURLRequest` objects represent a URL load request in a manner independent of protocol and URL scheme.

Finally, **Line 4** is the one that does the work of updating the UIWebView control.

```
webView.loadRequest(request)
```

On Your Own

You may notice that when the application first starts the UIWebView control is blank. You can't actually see anything until a URL is loaded. Can you figure out how to make it load to Google on startup?

We don't do any validation on the text entered by the user. The user needs to write out the whole thing, including http://. If the user enters text starting with www. could you add the **http://** automatically?

How else can you make this better? (Hint: In the next chapter we'll cover how to store data permanently in an app-- such as saving a home page as a setting.)

21

Saving Data between Sessions

Introduction

One of the things that users expect is to be able to save their settings in an application and have those settings available when they come back to use the application at a later date. Think of the Apple weather application; it allows you to select the cities you are interested in and when you return to the application later those cities are still selected. Users expect it.

NSUserDefaults

One of the easier ways to store data is to use something called NSUserDefaults. There are, of course, other ways to save data for your application but this is a great place to start. Some are easy to use, but rather limited, while others are much harder to use, but give you a lot more capabilities. NSUserDefaults is on the easy, but limited end of the spectrum.

It has its limitations, but it is very easy to use, and is ideal for simple storage of things like Strings and numbers. The six types of things that you can store using NSUserDefaults are:

- NSData
- NSString
- NSNumber

- NSDate
- NSArray
- NSDictionary

Reading and Writing Values into NSUserDefaults

The simplest way to think of using NSUserDefaults is to set an object and to read an object. To set the object, use the **.setObject** method which takes two parameters: 1) the value you are storing and 2) the key you will use to identify the value later when you need to read it.

For example, to save the value "Boston" into the key of "City" you would use the following code:

```
NSUserDefaults.standardUserDefaults().setObject("Boston", forKey: "City")
```

To read the value of a previously-saved key, use the .objectForKey method, such as:

```
var homeCity = NSUserDefaults.standardUserDefaults().objectForKey("City")
print (homeCity)
```

In the code above I declare a variable called homeCity then read the previously-saved value using the key of "City". In the next line I just print out the value but of course you could do much more, such as write it to the screen or pass it as a parameter to another function for further processing.

Note that if the key you are searching for is not found, then objectForKey will return a nil value, so you should definitely handle that case by wrapping it in a try/catch block.

Advanced Use Cases

If you were building a weather application you would likely rather store an array of cities, not just a single one. Luckily you can store an array in NSUserDefaults as well, it just takes a bit more work.

Saving an Array

Let's say your application lets the user add any number of cities to a list, and that you now wish to store that list.   First, put the cities into an array, such as follows:

```
let array = ["Boston", "London", "Paris", "Hyderabad"]
```

Next, we will save the array into the NSUserDefaults:

```
NSUserDefaults.standardUserDefaults().setObject(array, forKey: "Cities")
```

Reading an Array

To retrieve the array from the NSUserDefaults use the following code as an example:

```
let returnedArray =
NSUserDefaults.standardUserDefaults().objectForKey("Cities") as! NSArray
```

Note that I put an exclamation point after the as! because otherwise Swift with choke on it. The exclamation point states that we are sure that it can be converted from an object to an array. We can then easily then loop through the array as follows:

```
for x in returnedArray{
    print (x)
}
```

22

Multi-Screen Applications

Introduction

Most of the applications you see in the real world offer more than just a single screen. Even the most basic application usually has some kind of settings page where you can customize the application to your liking. For example, if we wanted to extend the web browser application from the chapter Working with the UIWebView Control one of the things we might want to add is to allow the user to set their own home page.

This is accomplished by adding additional View Controllers to your program, and giving the users a way switch between the various views.   One view controller would be for the main program while another would be used to store the user's preferences using the techniques covered in the chapter Saving Data between Sessions

Adding A Second View Controller

To add a second View Controller to a project type the word view into the search box in the list of controls:

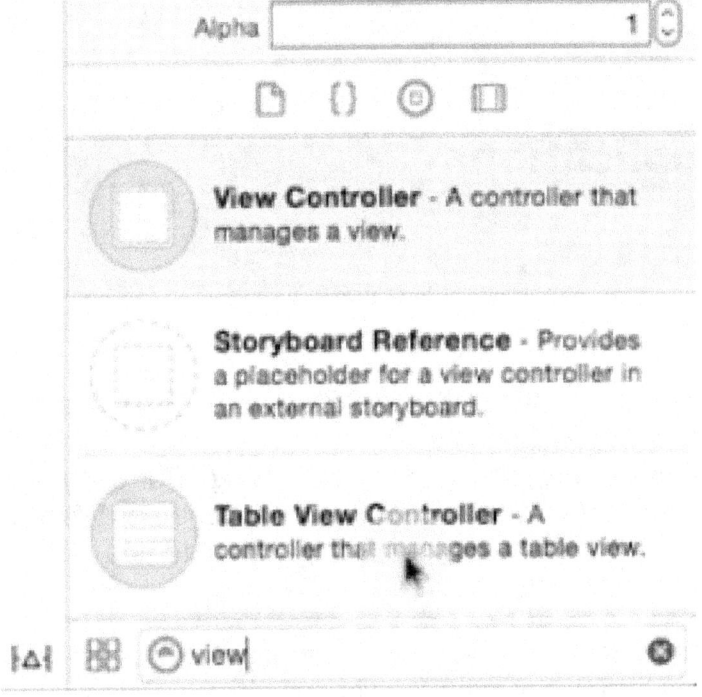

Grab the control and drag it onto your storyboard.

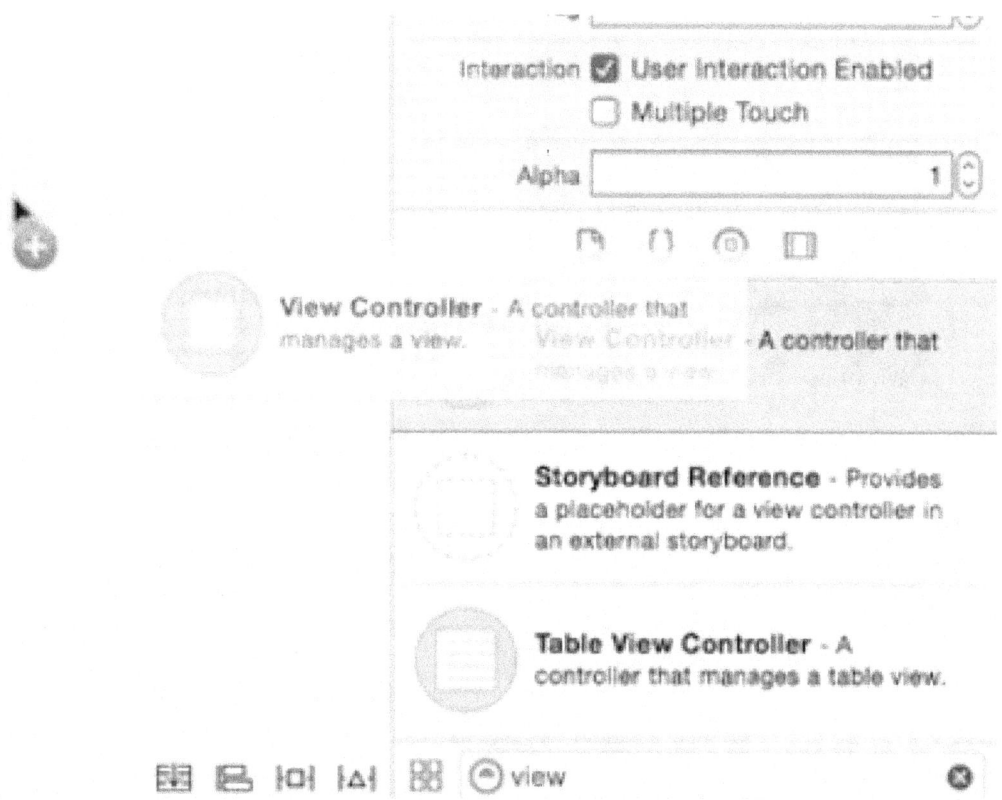

At this point you should have two view controllers side by side. So how do you get the user from one screen to another? This is actually very easy to do and doesn't even require any coding. You just need a button on each screen so each screen can get to the other.

Then select one of the buttons and control drag to the other View Controller that you want the button to link to. When you let go of the button you'll be presented with the Action Segue dialog box:

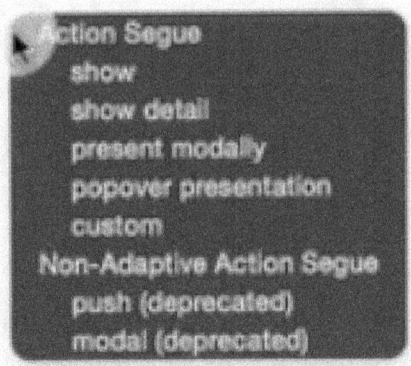

If you select the option "present modally" the screen will switch from the first View Controller to the other.   So the users have an option to get back, you'll need to create a second segue for the opposite direction.

23

Navigation Bars and Toolbars

Introduction

A common way to help your users navigate your application is to use a Navigation Bar or a Toolbar. A Navigation Bar sits across the **top** of an application and provides a number of possible actions to the user. For example, the Clock app included with iOS features a navigation bar at the top of the Alarms tab to allow the user to **add** an alarm (by pressing the + button) and to **edit** an existing alarm (by pressing the text 'Edit').

The navigation bar also features the text 'Alarm' centered, to help the user keep track of where they are inside the app.

Toolbar

A toolbar is similar to a navigation bar, except it sits at the bottom of the screen rather than the top. Again in the Clock app, a toolbar is featured at the bottom of the screen, to let you switch between the various modules in the Clock app.   Of course, what's really happening in that application is that it is switching between view controllers, as covered in the chapter Multi-Screen Applications.

Sample Application

In this chapter we'll be building a simple application with a navigation bar across the top and a toolbar on the bottom:

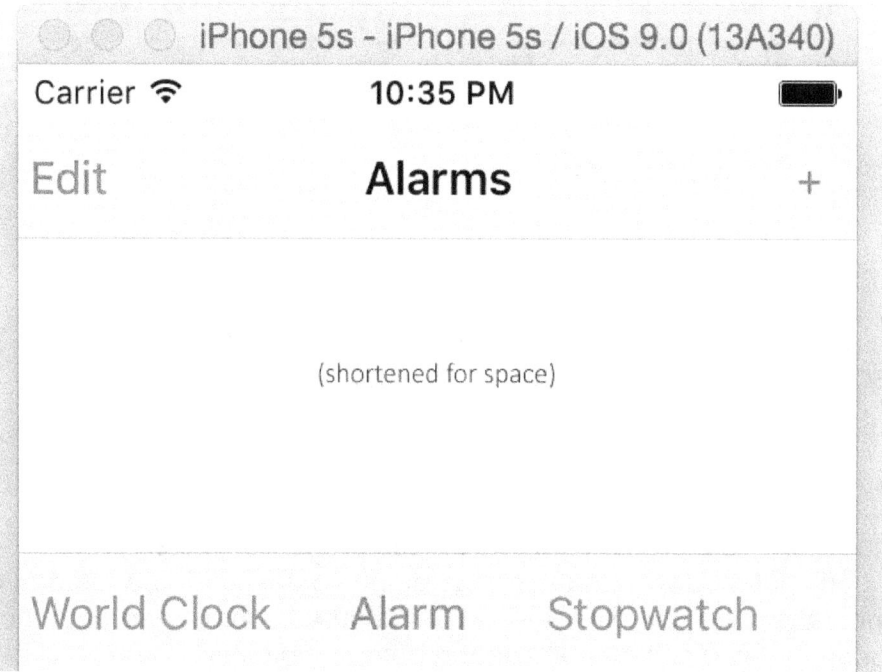

Adding A Navigation Bar control

To add a navigation bar to your storyboard, search for the navigation bar control then drag it onto the workspace.

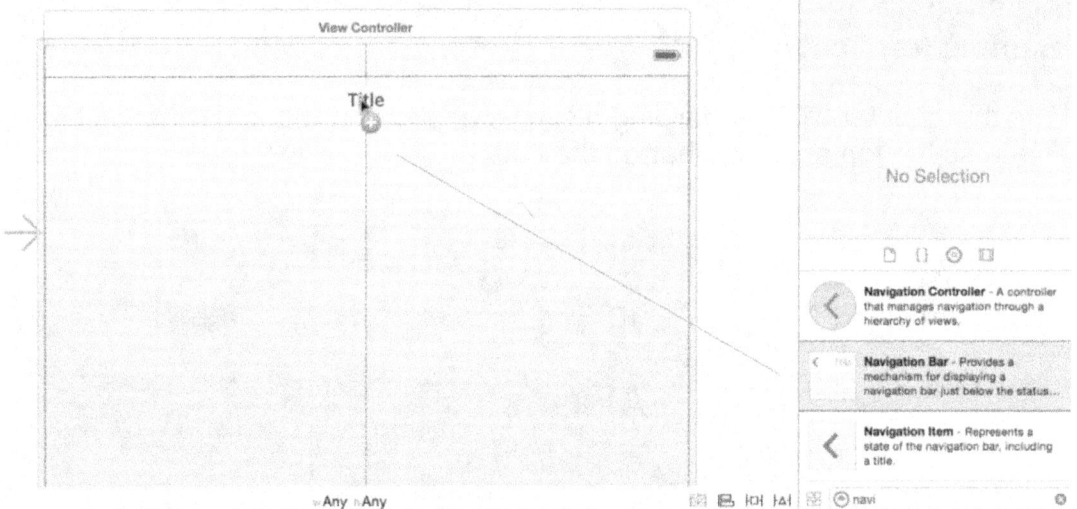

You can double click on the bar itself to change the text from the default "Title" to something that make sense for your application.

Placing the Navigation Bar

The navigation bar should generally be placed at the top of the screen. However, don't put it **flush** with the top as doing so obscures the general icon bar with the battery life and other indicators. Instead leave a gap of 20 pixels or so, enough that you can clearly see the battery indicator.

Next add some constraints for the navigation bar so that it will look nice across different devices and also if the device orientation changes. Select the navigation bar then click the Add Constraints button on the bottom. It's the button that looks like a Star Wars TIE fighter to me, and is circled in the screen shot below:

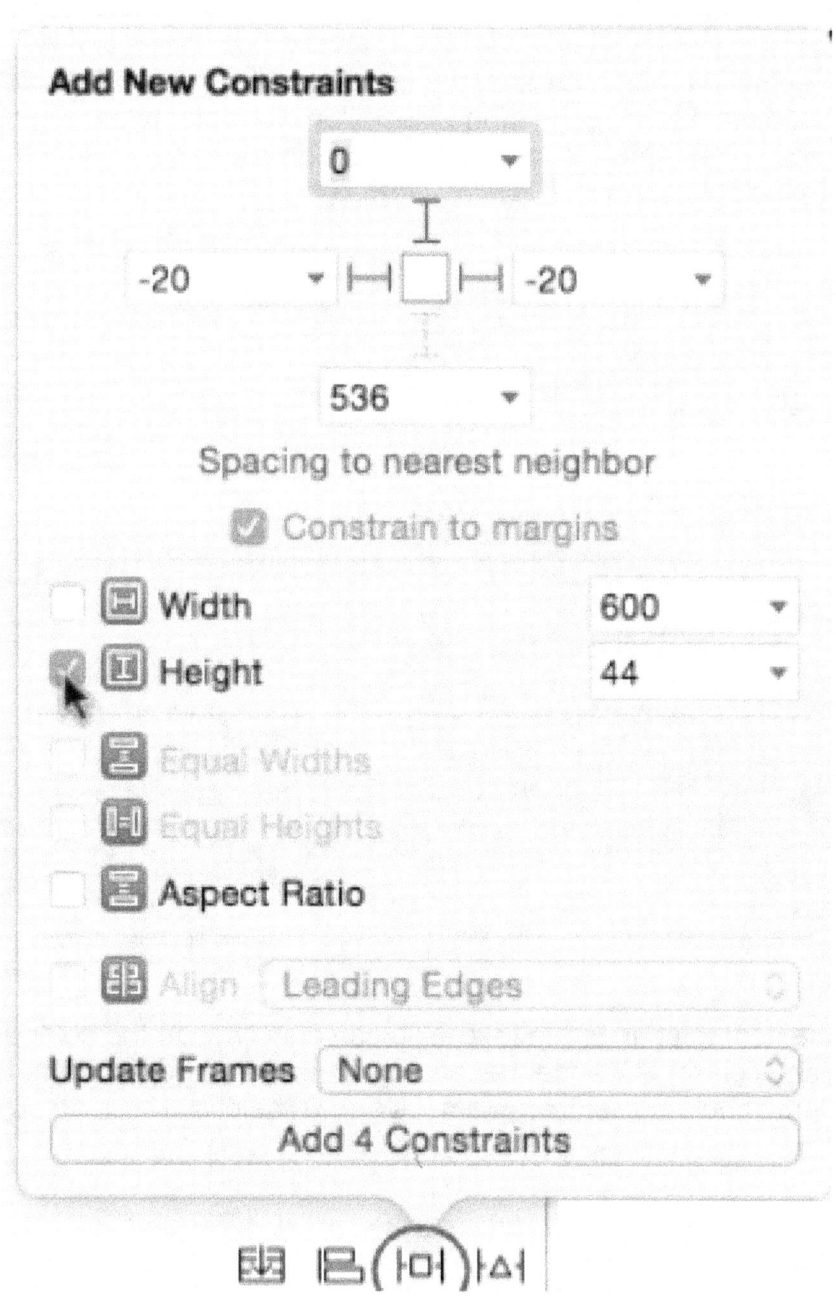

Select constraints for the top, sides, and height.

Adding Bar Button Items

Next we'll add items to the bar. Search the list of controls for **Bar Button Item**. To duplicate the Alarms page of the clock app, we'll add two actions, one on each side. First, drag a control to the left side of the screen, then drag another to the right side.

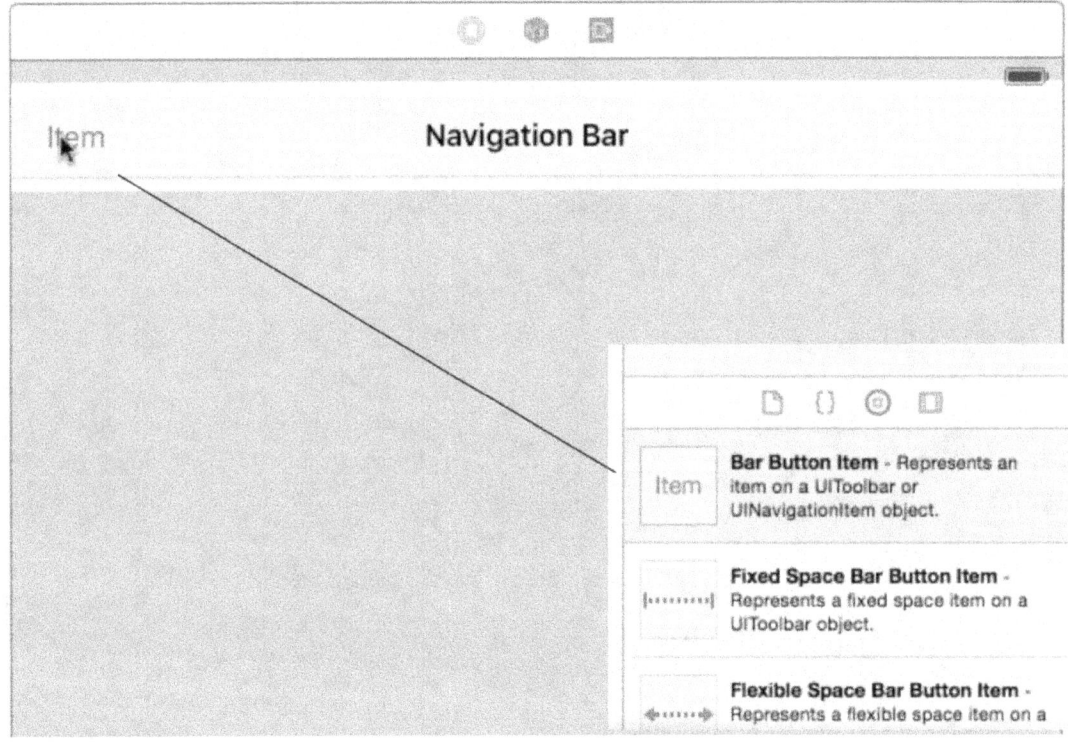

Double-click the item to change the text. You can also change the color as you would on any control. Change the left side to Edit and the right side to +. The System Item should be set to custom, as shown below:

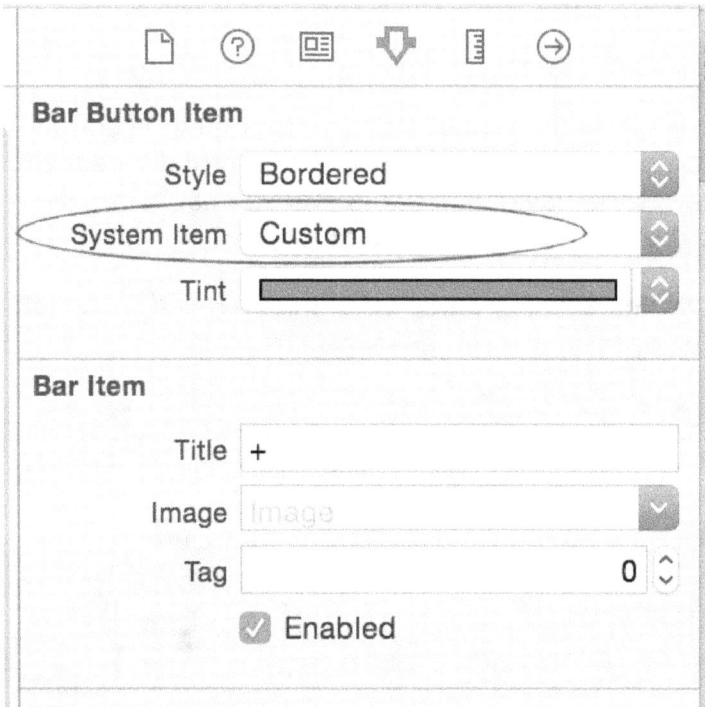

From the System Item drop-down you can also select from a number of pre-defined icons, such as camera, search, play, etc. Play around with the various options. You can also use a custom icon by selecting from the Image option to select from images you have already added to the project.

Adding A Toolbar

Adding a toolbar is very similar to the process above. Search the controls for toolbar, then drag it to the bottom of the screen. The only real difference in the behavior of the toolbar vs the navigation bar is that you can't drag items to the right side. Instead they all go to the left automatically.

If you want to position your items in any place other than aligned to the left you need to use one of the space bar controls.

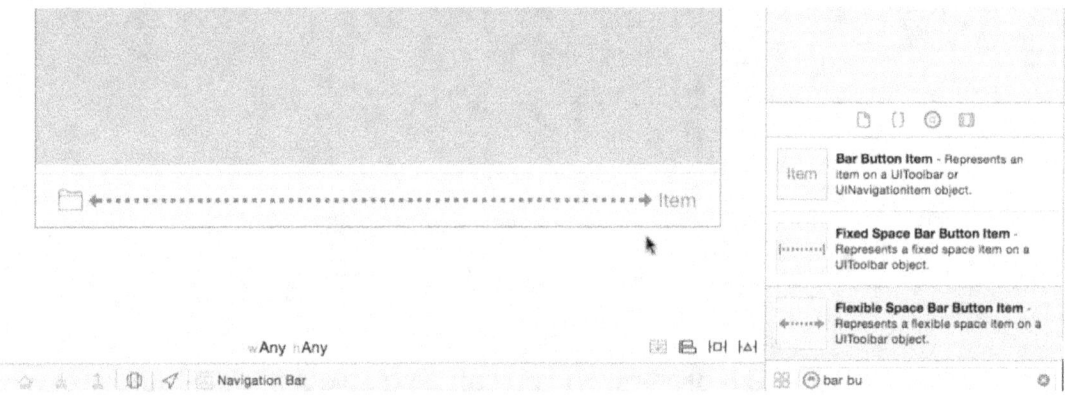

Use the **Fixed** Space Bar Button item to insert a variable amount of space between items. You drag it between buttons then you can size it as you like. The **Flexible** Space Bar Button Item (shown above) automatically stretches to fill all the available between the buttons. If you have three buttons and place a flexible spacer between each you will end up with a button on the left, center, and right.

24

Keyboard Tricks

Introduction

Most applications you write will use the keyboard in one way or another. While this is something we take for granted as just appearing when needed, the problem is that the keyboard generally does not disappear when not needed. That is left to the developer to decide.

Option 1: Touch outside a text area

The first way to get rid of the keyboard when you are done with it is to touch somewhere on the screen outside the next input area.

```
override func touchesBegan(touches: Set<UITouch>, withEvent event: UIEvent?) {
    self.view.endEditing(true)
}
```

Option 2: Hide keyboard on Return key

The next way to get rid of the keyboard is to hide it when the user presses the Return key. This is slightly trickier because the solution involves more than code. Put the following code in your app:

```
func textFieldShouldReturn(textField: UITextField) -> Bool {
    textBox.resignFirstResponder()
    return true
}
```

For it to work you need to declare a delegate for the text box that the user will be typing into. Do that by dragging from the text box to the view controller icon then select delegate.

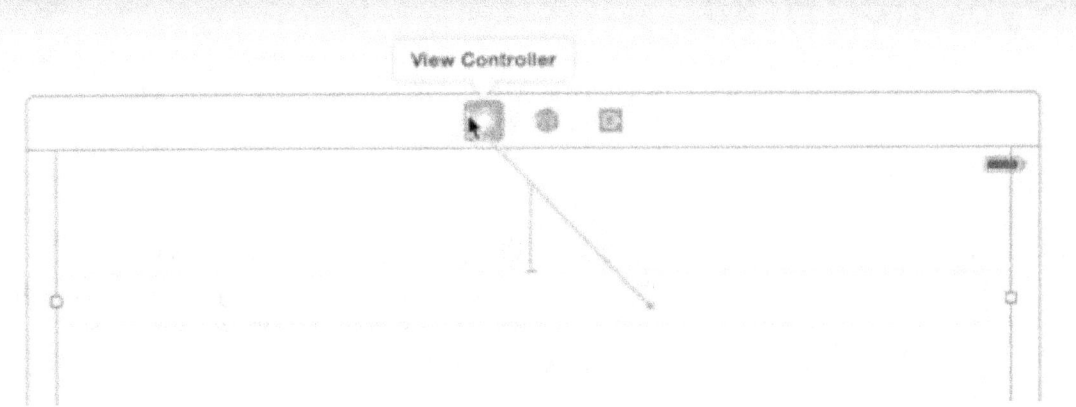

25

Working with Maps

Introduction

The proliferation of map data has enabled thousands of cool applications that incorporate mapping information into mobile applications. Apple has its own map data and API and that information can be easily accessed from within Swift using something called the MapKit. Let's build a basic application using maps.

A Quick Refresher on Latitude and Longitude

Latitude and longitude are used to uniquely define locations on the earth.

Latitude is a series of parallel circles which run east to west. Latitude is defined with respect to distance from the equator. If the point is above the equator the latitude number is positive (or north). If the point is below the equator, the latitude number is negative (or southerly). Latitude can range up to positive 90 degrees (or 90 degrees north), and down to negative 90 degrees (or 90 degrees south). Thus Latitudes of +90 and -90 correspond to the north and south poles, respectively.

Longitude is a series of parallel circles which run north to south and is defined in terms of meridians, which are half-circles running from pole to pole. The prime meridian is the reference point from which longitude is measured. The prime meridian passes through Greenwich, England and so it is also referred to as the Greenwich meridian. If a point is to the west of the prime meridian, the longitude number is negative and if it is to the east is positive. Longitude numbers can range up to positive180 degrees (180 degrees east), and down to negative180 degrees (180 degrees west). The +180 and -180 degree longitude meridians coincide directly opposite the prime meridian.

Longitude and Latitude are expressed in units called degrees.   Because the earth is a sphere, the difference between one degree and another varies depending on where on earth it is. In other words a degree of longitude is longest at the equator and gets progressively smaller the further away from the equator you go.

Sample Application

In this chapter we'll be building a simple application that allows the user to view a map.

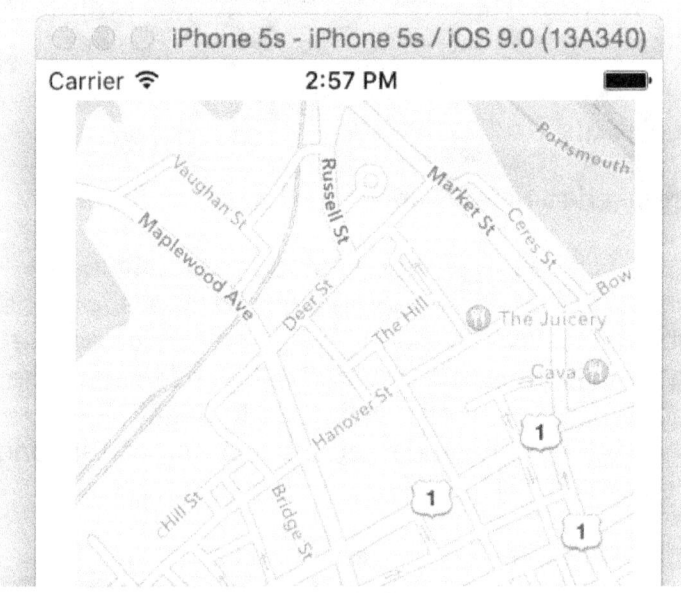

Adding A Map Control

To add a control to your storyboard, search for the map control then drag it onto the storyboard.

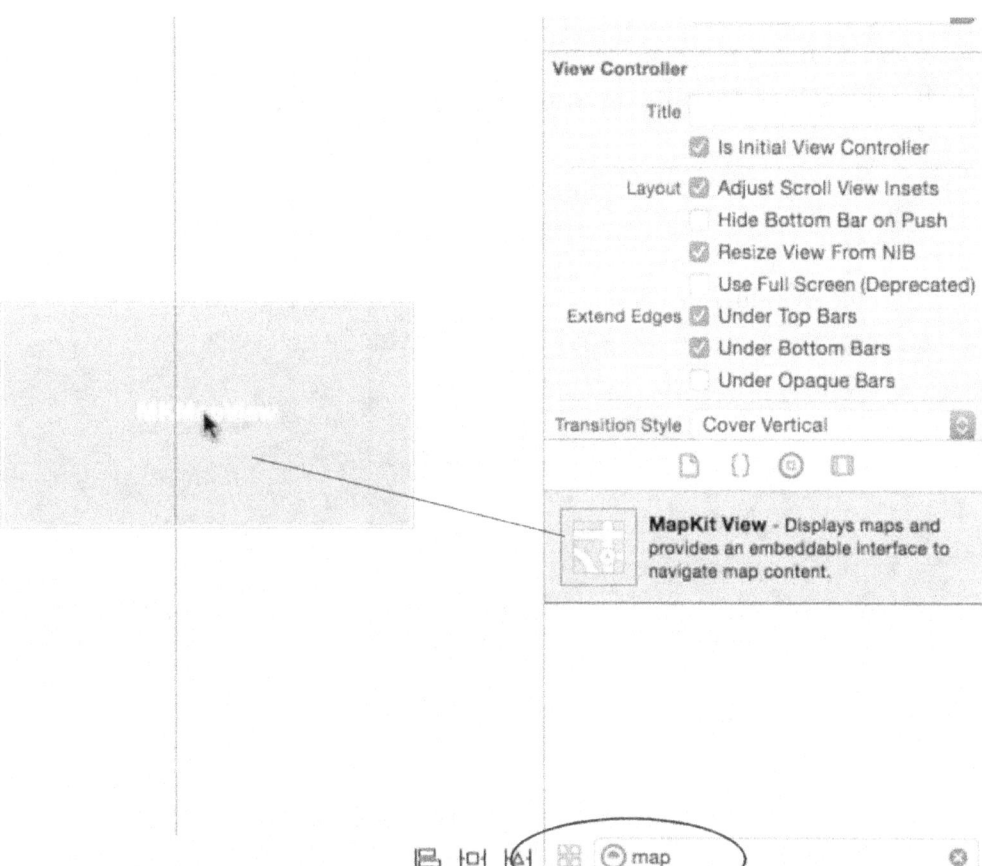

Next display the code view and view controller side by side so that you can create an Outlet for the map. Do this by control-dragging from the map to the code. Position the component to look nice then click the "TIE fighter" control in the bottom right to add the missing constraints so the map will stay where you want to appear.

At this point you cannot yet run the app; a bit of code is required first. After the line that says **import UIKit** add a line that says **import MapKit**. This enables you to access the features built into Apple's map framework. Any function that is part of the MapKit framework will start with the letters MK.

Also, you need to modify the line that starts with class ViewController: to also have the MKMapViewDelegate. This delegate allows our view controller to control the map component.

Your code window should now look similar to this:

```
import UIKit
import MapKit
class ViewController: UIViewController, MKMapViewDelegate {
    @IBOutlet weak var map: MKMapView!
    override func viewDidLoad() {
        super.viewDidLoad()
        // Do any additional setup after loading the view, typically from a nib.
    }
}
```

At this point you should be able to run the app, although it won't do much yet.

Specifying the Map Starting Location and Zoom Level

Map coordinates are specified using longitude and latitude. To use the map control you'll need to specify the center location (in latitude and longitude) and also specify how "zoomed in" the map is by specifying the width and height of the map as the number of degrees in latitude and longitude respectfully.

To specify all these attributes requires a number of variables. I'll work backwards through the hierarchy of what the map component requires. To initialize a map you pass it a **region**, and specify whether you want it to be animated or not.

```
map.setRegion (region, animated: Boolean)
```

A map **region** consists of a starting location (the center of the map) and a span (the edges of the map). To create a region you call a method called MKCoordinateRegionMake and pass it two parameters. You guessed it, those two parameters are a **starting location** and a **span**. Both of these parameters are actually *objects* that have to be first created by calling their respective xxxMake methods. Let's talk a bit about these two objects:

The **starting location** is specified as a 2D coordinate and is created using the method CLLocationCoordinate2dMake. Methods that start with CL are referencing the core location (CL) framework. Generally any framework that starts with C does not require an import statement because it is part of the "core" set of functions built into Swift.

Anyway, CLLocationCoordinate2dMake takes a latitude and a longitude as its parameters, which are expressed in degrees.

```
CLLocatonCoordinate2DMake (latitude, longitude)
```

The **span** specifies how much area around the starting location is displayed. A span is made up of two "deltas". In mathematics, a delta refers to the difference between two variables. In the context of Apple maps it means the difference in degrees (of latitude or longitude) from the left side of the map to the right side (degrees latitude) and from the top of the map to the bottom of the map (degrees longitude.) In other words you need to specify the delta (or difference) in degrees from one side of the map to the other side.

To specify a span you use the method MKCoordinateSpanMake, which takes two **deltas** as its parameters.

I know this seems like a lot, but we're almost at the end. Deltas are expressed in degrees of longitude and latitude. Locations are expressed as a pair of points, also expressed in degrees of longitude and latitude.

So to get started we need four variables which contain degrees: the latitude and longitude of our starting point and the delta of degrees for each. So we'll create four variables of type CLLocationDegrees, as follows:

```
1.   var latitude: CLLocationDegrees = 43.0756
2.   var longitude: CLLocationDegrees = -70.7606
3.   var latDelta: CLLocationDegrees = 0.01
4.   var longDelta: CLLocationDegrees = 0.01
```

Line 1 is the *latitude* of our starting point. **Line 2** is the *longitude* of our starting point. These two points together specify the center of Portsmouth, New Hampshire, USA. **Line 3** is the number of degrees in latitude from the left side of the map to the right side. **Line 4** is the number of degrees in longitude from the top of the map to the bottom.

Next we need to create a span. Recall that map takes a region as its parameter and a region is made up of a starting location and a span. So the next thing we need is those two pieces. Let's start with a span:

```
var span: MKCoordinateSpan = MKCoordinateSpanMake(latDelta, longDelta)
```

Here we have created a variable named **span** which is of the type MKCoordinateSpan. We assign it a value by using MKCoordinateSpan**Make** function and passing it our two deltas, latDelta and longDelta.

Next we need to create the starting location.

```
var location:CLLocationCoordinate2D = CLLocationCoordinate2DMake(latitude, longitude)
```

Here we have created a variable named **location** which is of the type CLLocationCoordinate2D. We assign it a value using CLLocationCoordinate2D**Make** and passing it our two variables latitude and longitude.

Finally we can create the region because we have both the starting location "location" and the span "span".

```
var region: MKCoordinateRegion = MKCoordinateRegionMake(location, span)
```

Now that we have a region properly defined, we can tell Swift to use this region to display the map the way we want it to appear.

```
map.setRegion(region, animated: true)
```

If all goes well your application should now run and look similar to this:

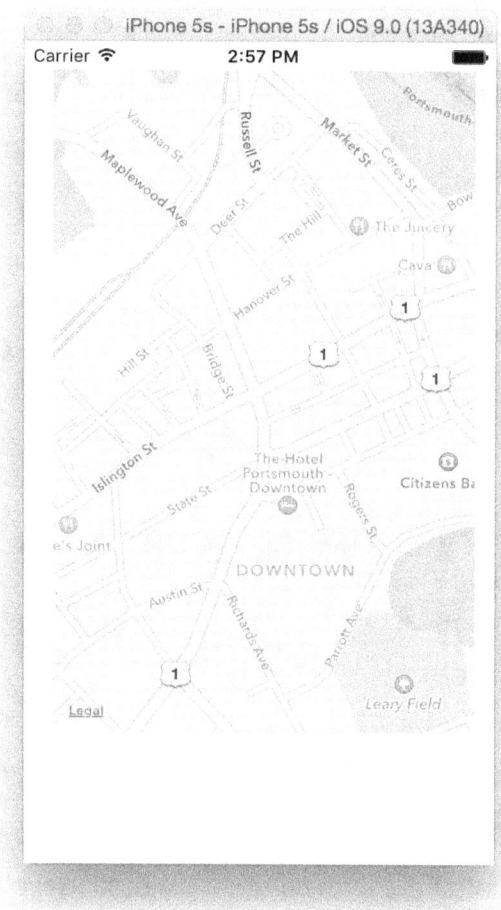

Adding Annotations in Code

Sometimes the point of a map is to highlight something in particular. The way to highlight a location is to put a pin on the map. Adding pins is actually pretty easy. Here is what we'll be building:

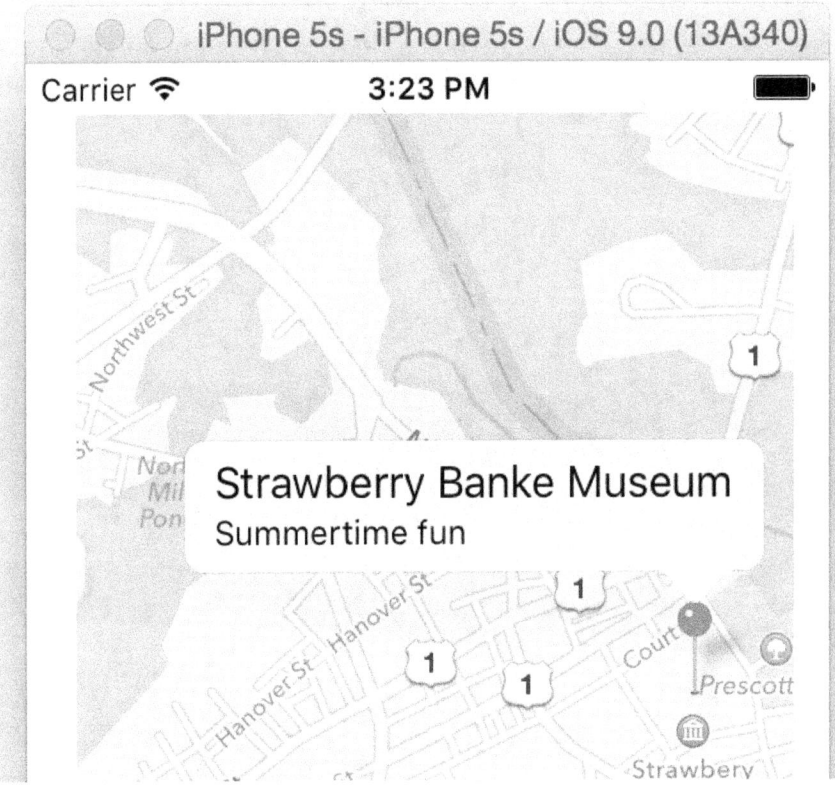

Apple refers to these pins as annotations. To create an annotation we'll use the following code:

```
1.    // Add an annotation
2.    var annotation = MKPointAnnotation()
3.    var parkLat: CLLocationDegrees = 43.075821
4.    var parkLong: CLLocationDegrees = -70.7532432
5.    var ParkLocation:CLLocationCoordinate2D =
```

```
           CLLocationCoordinate2DMake(parkLat, parkLong)
6.         annotation.coordinate = ParkLocation
7.         annotation.title = "Strawberry Banke Museum"
8.         annotation.subtitle = "Summertime fun"
9.         map.addAnnotation(annotation)
```

On **Line 1** we add a comment describing what the next bit of code will do. It's always a good practice to add comments throughout your code. On **Line 2** we create a variable called annotation of type MKPointAnnotation. On **Lines 3 - 4** we create two variables to hold the longitude and latitude of the location where we want the pin to go. In **Line 5** we create a coordinate using the latitude and longitude. This is the same technique we used to create the center point of our map.

On **Line 7** you specify the *title* of the annotation, which will appear if the user clicks on the pin. On **Line 8** we create the *subtitle* and finally, on **Line 9,** we add the annotation to the map.

User Annotations

Sometimes you want the map to display annotations that you set, sometimes you may want the end user to be able to add an annotation. This is also reasonably easy to accomplish with the following code which would be added to the viewDidLoad() function:

```
1.    //Allow to user to drop a pin using a long press
2.    var uilpgr = UILongPressGestureRecognizer(target: self, action: "action:")
3.    uilpgr.minimumPressDuration = 2
4.    map.addGestureRecognizer(uilpgr)
```

Line 2 creates a variable called uilpgr which is an abbreviation of its type, which is the UILongPressGestureRecognizer. As you might guess, the UILongPressGestureRecognizer recognizes the gesture made by the user when they press and hold (long press) on the screen. UILongPressGestureRecognizer takes two parameters, 1) the target (where the gesture comes from, in this case **self** which is shorthand for the current ViewController and 2) what action to take when the gesture is recognized. In this case we are referring the gesture to a new function, aptly called "action".

Note that the name of the function (action) is followed by a **colon**.

This is one of those Swift quirks that can drive you crazy. If you don't add the colon the function will still be called, but it won't pass on any information, such as where on the screen the press occurred. So, just make sure you include the colon.

Next you need to write the function telling Swift what to do when the gesture is recognized. We do this with the following code:

```
1.      func action (gestureRecognizer: UIGestureRecognizer)
2.   {
3.         let touchPoint = gestureRecognizer.locationInView(self.map)
4.         let pinCoordinate: CLLocationCoordinate2D = map.convertPoint(touchPoint,
                 toCoordinateFromView: self.map)
5.         let annotation = MKPointAnnotation()
6.         annotation.coordinate = pinCoordinate
7.         annotation.title = "Dropped Pin"
8.         map.addAnnotation(annotation)
9.       }
```

In **Line 1** I declare the function called **action** and specify that it takes a parameter of *UIGestureRecognizer*, which will be referred to in the function using the variable named **gesturerecognizer**. In **Line 3** I get what is called a "touch point". This is the point on the screen where the user touched, but it is a screen coordinate not a map coordinate. In **Line 4** I create a variable called **pinCoordinate** which is a map point (technically, it's a *CLLocationCoordinate2D*). I set the value of the map point using the convenient method **convertPoint**, which takes two parameters: 1) the point that was touched as captured in the variable **touchPoint**, and 2) the thing that was touched (in this case the map).

The rest is exactly the same as creating the annotation in code; the only difference is that we got the location from the user instead of specifying it.

Code

```swift
// ViewController.swift
// MapInfo
//
// Created by Alan Forbes
// Copyright © 2015 Alan Forbes. All rights reserved.
//

import UIKit
import MapKit

class ViewController: UIViewController, MKMapViewDelegate,CLLocationManagerDelegate {

    @IBOutlet weak var map: MKMapView!

    override func viewDidLoad() {
        super.viewDidLoad()
        let latitude: CLLocationDegrees = 43.0756
        let longitude: CLLocationDegrees = -70.7606
        let latDelta: CLLocationDegrees = 0.02
        let longDelta: CLLocationDegrees = 0.02

        var span: MKCoordinateSpan = MKCoordinateSpanMake(latDelta, longDelta)
        var location:CLLocationCoordinate2D = CLLocationCoordinate2DMake(latitude,
longitude)
        var region: MKCoordinateRegion = MKCoordinateRegionMake(location, span)
        map.setRegion(region, animated: true)

        // Add an annotation via code
        var annotation = MKPointAnnotation()
        var parkLat: CLLocationDegrees = 43.075821
        var parkLong: CLLocationDegrees = -70.7532432
        var ParkLocation:CLLocationCoordinate2D = CLLocationCoordinate2DMake(parkLat,
parkLong)
        annotation.coordinate = ParkLocation
        annotation.title = "Strawberry Banke Museum"
        annotation.subtitle = "Summertime fun"
```

```swift
        map.addAnnotation(annotation)

        //Allow to user to drop a pin using a long press
        var uilpgr = UILongPressGestureRecognizer(target: self, action: "action:")
        uilpgr.minimumPressDuration = 2
        map.addGestureRecognizer(uilpgr)

    }

    func action (gesturerecognizer: UIGestureRecognizer) {
        let touchPoint = gesturerecognizer.locationInView(self.map)
        let pinCoordinate: CLLocationCoordinate2D = map.convertPoint(touchPoint,
toCoordinateFromView: self.map)
        let annotation = MKPointAnnotation()
        annotation.coordinate = pinCoordinate
        annotation.title = "Dropped Pin"
        map.addAnnotation(annotation)

    }

    override func didReceiveMemoryWarning() {
        super.didReceiveMemoryWarning()
        // Dispose of any resources that can be recreated.
    }

}
```

26

Geolocation

Introduction

Many Apple devices have built-in GPS and those that don't can usually figure out their location surprisingly well just by measuring the relative strengths of the various WiFi networks which are within range.   If you want to build an application that is aware of the user's location, this is the right chapter. We will extend our map application from the previous chapter to show the user's location as the center of the map.

Setup and Permissions Required!

An application cannot access the user's location without permission. This takes a bit of setup.   First you need to bring in the **Core Location** framework, which is easily confused with but not the same as CLLocationXXX stuff we used in the previous chapter-- that being Core Libary.

Adding the Core Location framework

To add the core location framework you select on the name of your project in the top left corner, then click on Build Phases, and then on Link Binary with Library. To help make this easy to follow, I labeled each step with 1, 2, 3 in the image that follows.

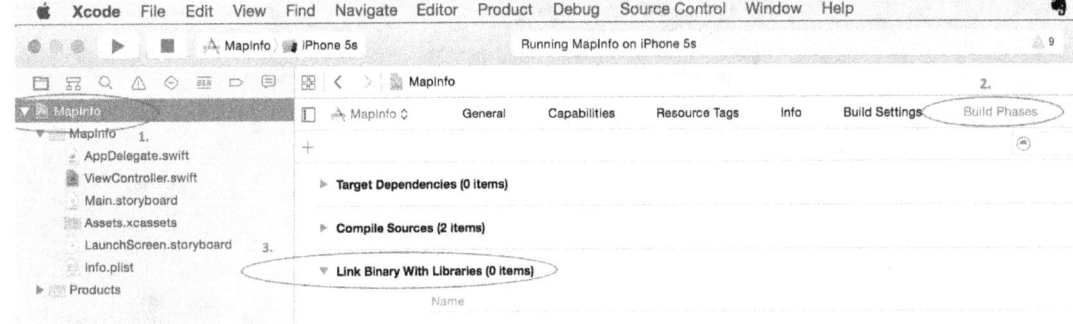

Next click on the plus button underneath Link Binary and then search for location, select it and click **Add**.

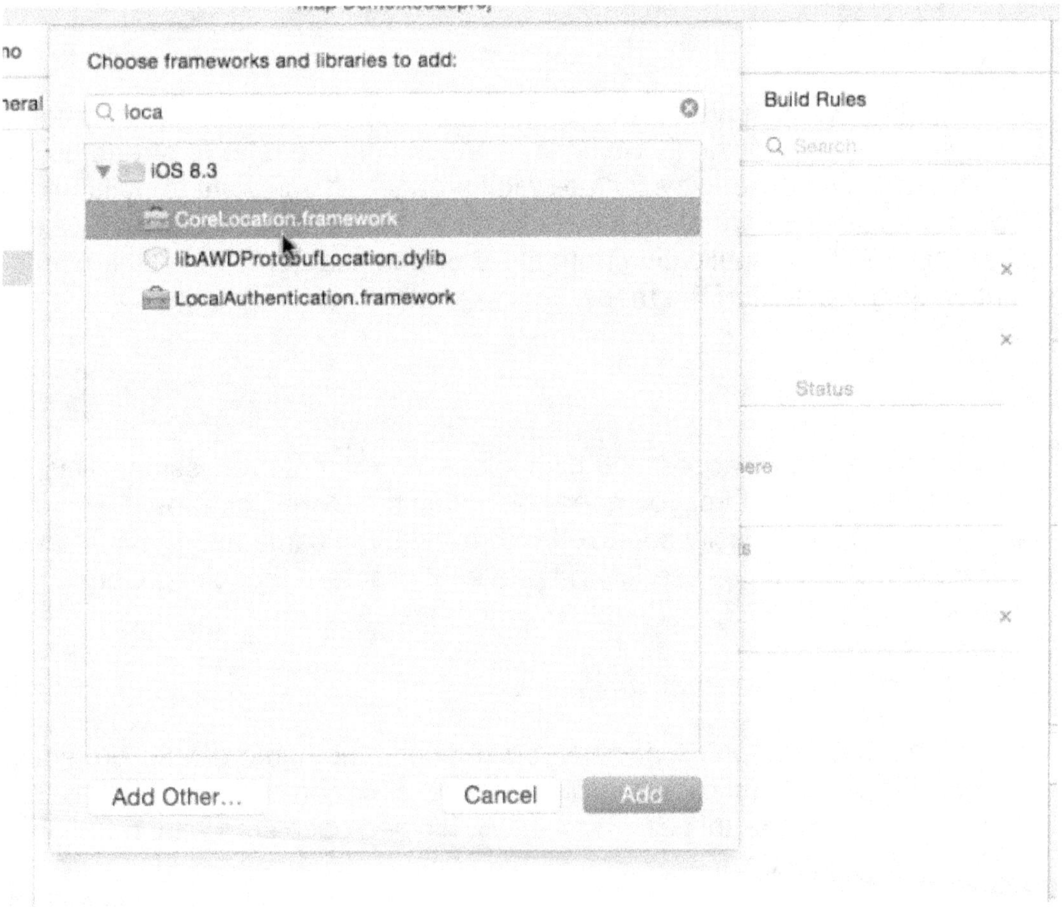

Adding the Permission Strings

Next we need to provide the text that the application will use when asking the user for permission to access the location. Under your project in the left file navigator will be a folder called Supporting Files and inside that is a file called "Info.plist".

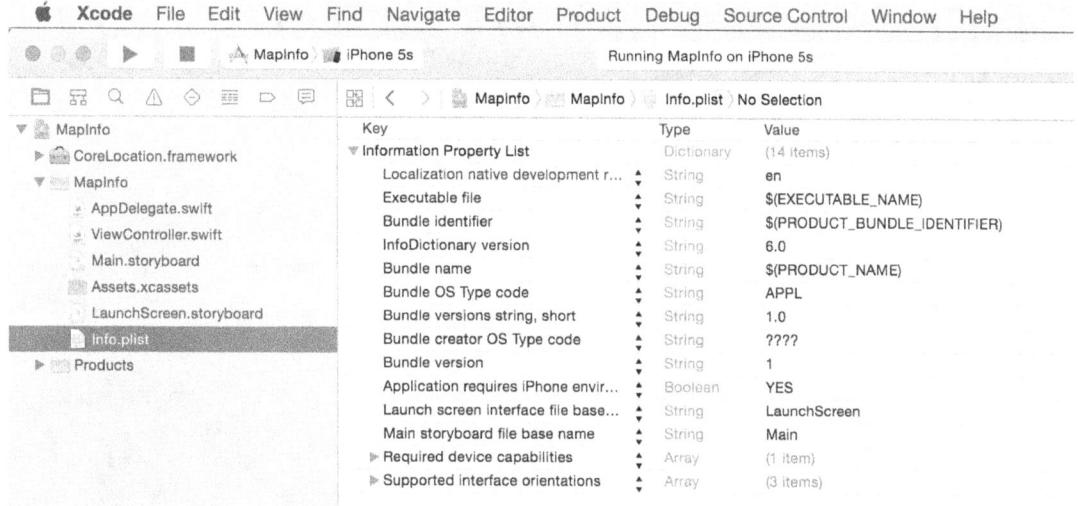

When you click on that file you'll see a set of keyword/value pairs and as you mouse over the items you'll see plus and a minus icons appear. The minus lets you remove the highlighted row while the plus lets you insert a new row at the cursor position.

We need to add two rows: one for asking the user for permission to access the location while the application is **in use** and one for asking the user for permission to access the location while the application is **in the background**.

The first key is NSLocationWhenInUseUsageDescription and the second key is NSLocationAlwaysUsageDescription. These keys are paired with strings that you enter and theoretically can contain any message you wish but know that Apple will see them if you submit your application to the app store. For the first value (NSLocationWhenInUseUsageDescription) I added the string *"While the application is running the map will be updated."* This is a good example of a descriptor because it describes a reason why the end user should allow the access.

For the second key (NSLocationAlwaysUsageDescription) I entered the snarky *"While the application is in the background we want to spy on you."* A user presented with this justification for allowing an application access to location data will probably decline and if Apple sees a message like that they will likely reject your application from the app store.

Adding the CLLocatonManagerDelegate

The last bit of setup involves adding CLLocatonManagerDelegate to the view controller class and import CoreLocation so that the top of the class looks like this, with the new parts on lines 3 and Line 4

```
1.    import UIKit
2.    import MapKit
3.    import CoreLocation
4.    class ViewController: UIViewController, MKMapViewDelegate {
5.        @IBOutlet weak var map: MKMapView!
6.        override func viewDidLoad() {
7.            super.viewDidLoad()
8.            // Do any additional setup after loading the view, typically from a nib.
9.        }
10.   }
```

Start Coding

First create a variable to hold the location manager. You need to create this at the application level so that it can be accessed both in the start up routine and also from other functions. The new line is on shown on **Line 6**. If you put this line inside the viewDidLoad function you'll see the permissions box flash by too quickly to even answer.

```
1.    import UIKit
2.    import MapKit
3.    import CoreLocation
4.    class ViewController: UIViewController, MKMapViewDelegate {
5.        @IBOutlet weak var map: MKMapView!
6.        var locationManager = CLLocationManager()
7.
8.        override func viewDidLoad() {
9.            super.viewDidLoad()
10.           // Do any additional setup after loading the view, typically from a nib.
11.       }
12.   }
```

Updating viewDidLoad

We need to set some of the attributes of our locationManager and the best place to do that is on the load event of the view controller. Add the following 4 lines:

```
1.        locationManager.delegate = self
2.        locationManager.desiredAccuracy = kCLLocationAccuracyBest
3.        locationManager.requestWhenInUseAuthorization()
4.        locationManager.startUpdatingLocation()
```

Line 1 sets the locationManager's delegate to self. This is something that you seem to need to do a lot in Swift. **Line 2** sets the desired accuracy of the location. I recommend selecting the option "Accuracy Best" as this allows the device to fall back on alternate methods if the GPS is not available.

As shown in the next screen shot this is not something you should have to type but rather something you can select from available options:

```
class ViewController: UIViewController, MKMapViewDelegate,CLLocationManagerDelegate {

    @IBOutlet weak var map: MKMapView!

    override func viewDidLoad() {
        super.viewDidLoad()

        var locationManager = CLLocationManager()

        locationManager.delegate = self
        locationManager.desiredAccuracy = kCLLocationAccuracyBest
```

	CLLocationAccuracy	kCLLocationAccuracyBest
let la	CLLocationAccuracy	kCLLocationAccuracyBest
let lo	CLLocationAccuracy	kCLLocationAccuracyBestForNavigation
let la	CLLocationAccuracy	kCLLocationAccuracyHundredMeters
let lo	CLLocationAccuracy	kCLLocationAccuracyKilometer
var sp	CLLocationAccuracy	kCLLocationAccuracyNearestTenMeters
var lo	CLLocationAccuracy	kCLLocationAccuracyThreeKilometers |, longitu
var re	CLLocationCoordinate2D	kCLLocationCoordinate2DInvalid
map.se		

Use the highest-level of accuracy. <u>More...</u>

```
// Add an annotation via code
var annotation = MKPointAnnotation()
```

3. locationManager.requestWhenInUseAuthorization()

Line 3 tells the location manager to ask the user for permission to use their location information when the application is in use. At run time this will trigger a prompt similar to the one shown below. You will notice that the subtitle to this dialog box is the text you provided in the info.plist entry.

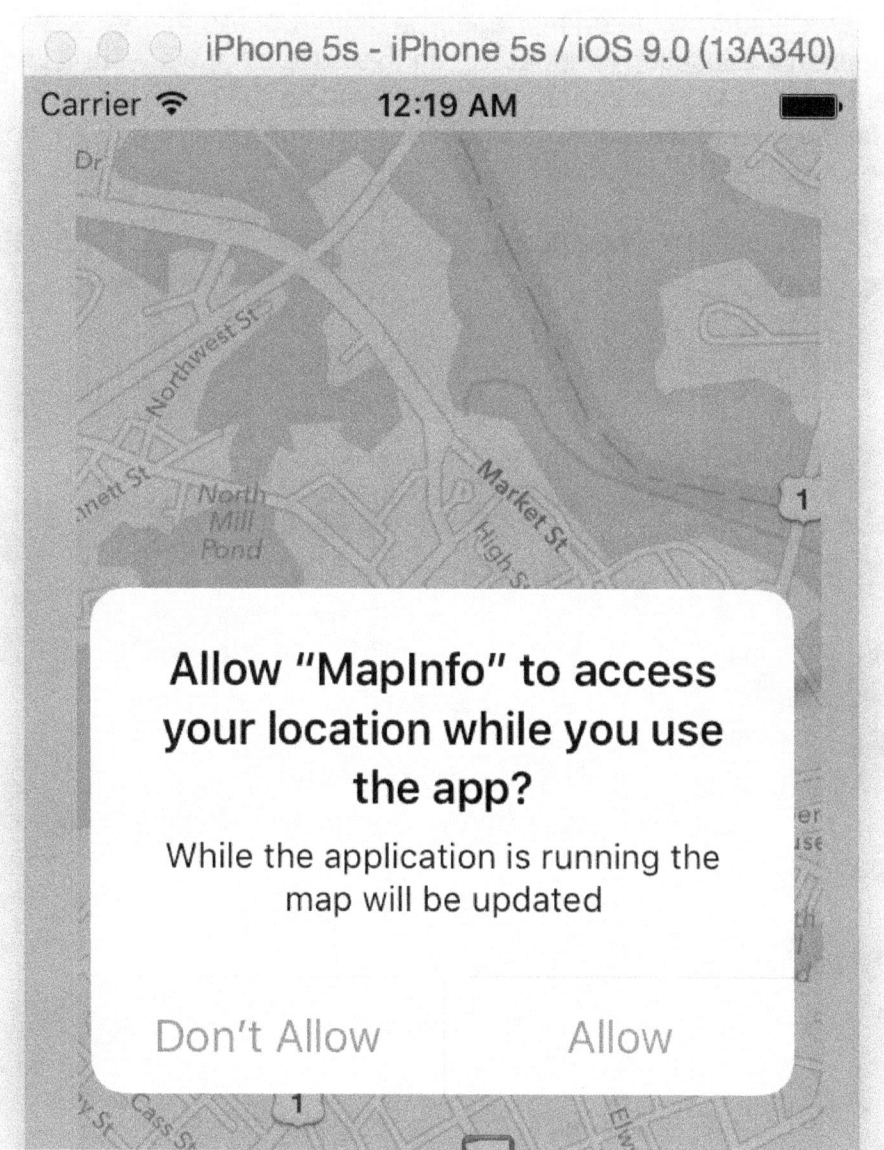

4. locationManager.startUpdatingLocation()

Line 4 tells the locatonManager to start collecting the user's location.

Add a Location Manager function

Next we'll add a location manager function that tells the application what to do when the location is updated. In this case what we want it to do is re-center the map. We can do this by converting the users location into latitude and longitude and using that information to build a map just as we did in the previous chapter.

```
1.      func locationManager(manager: CLLocationManager, didUpdateLocations
locations: [CLLocation]) {
2.
3.      var myUserLocation: CLLocation = locations[0]
4.      var latitude = myUserLocation.coordinate.latitude
5.      var longitude = myUserLocation.coordinate.longitude
6.
7.      let latDelta: CLLocationDegrees = 0.02
8.      let longDelta: CLLocationDegrees = 0.02
9.
10.     var span: MKCoordinateSpan = MKCoordinateSpanMake(latDelta,
longDelta)
11.     var location:CLLocationCoordinate2D =
CLLocationCoordinate2DMake(latitude, longitude)
12.     var region: MKCoordinateRegion = MKCoordinateRegionMake(location,
span)
13.        self.map.setRegion(region, animated: true)
14.     }
```

27

Working with Audio

Introduction

Of course, the original function of the iPod was to play music, and Apple devices since have excelled at this function. If you would like to add audio to your application, this is the chapter for you.

We'll be building an application with a play/pause button and a volume control.

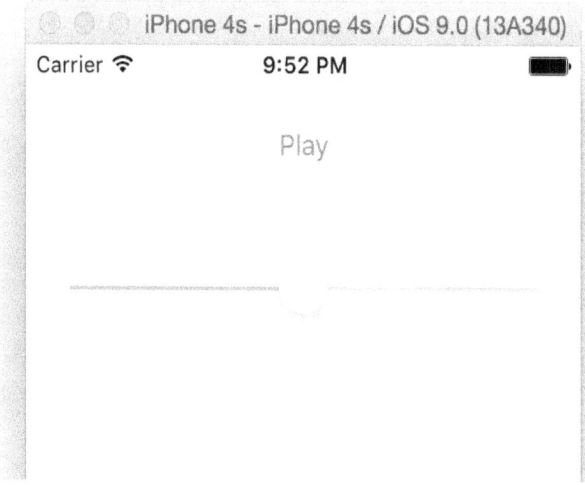

Build the User Interface

There's not much to this application, just a centered button and a centered slider control.   Label the button as **Play**. When the user clicks the button the sound file (music?) will start (play) and the label will change to Pause. Clicking the button again will pause the music and toggle the button label back.

Control drag from the two controls to create an outlet for each control:

@IBOutlet weak var playButton: UIButton!

@IBOutlet weak var sliderVolume: UISlider!

Add the Media

You'll need to select an MP3 file to use for your application. I chose an audio file of crashing waves and chose to name my application "Soothing Sounds" but you can use any MP3 file. Locate the desired file using Finder then drag it onto your project. Take the default values of the prompt but make sure you select "Copy items if needed".

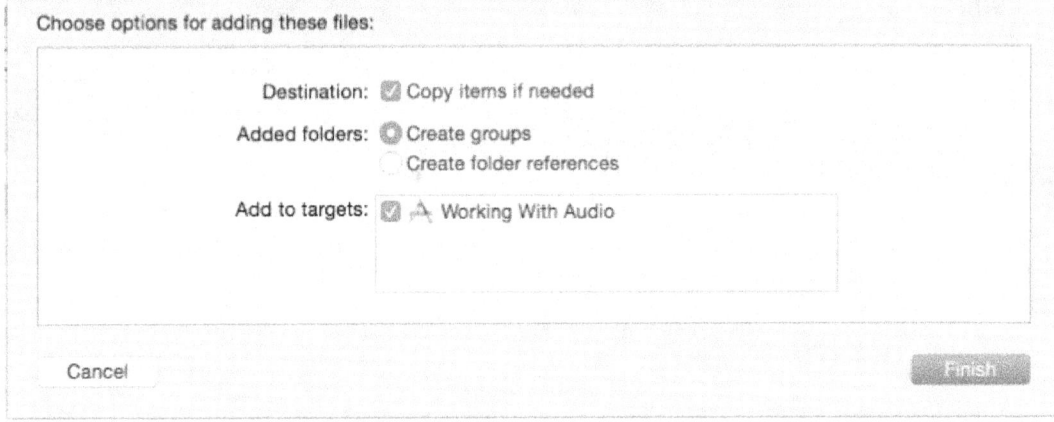

In my case the file I added was named "Ocean_Waves.mp3". If you successfully added it to your project it should look similar to the screen shot below:

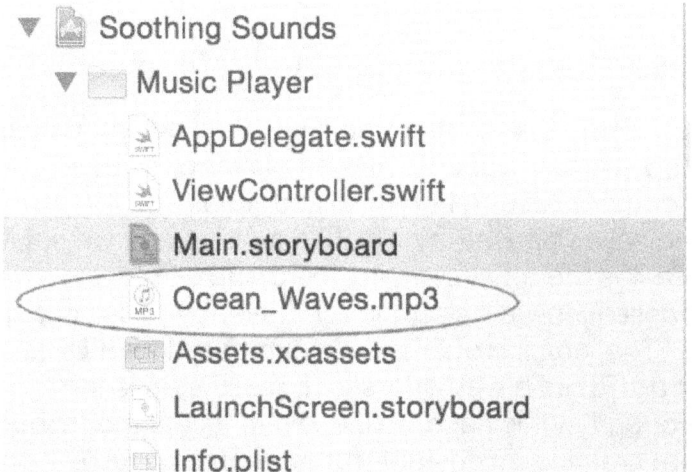

import AVFoundation

As you've seen with other projects, one of the first things you need to do is reference the appropriate library. In this case we'll be adding the Audio Visual Foundation framework. Find the line in your project that says import UIKit and add a line under it saying import AVFoundation:

import UIKit

import AVFoundation

Add Global Variables

Just after the line that starts with class ViewController, add three variables. The first will be the audio player component (which does not have a user interface so we can't just drag it onto the story board like we did with other components we've used so far), the second will be a variable we'll use to keep track of whether the button should say Play or Pause, and finally we'll create a variable to help the player locate the mp3 file we wish to play.

```
1.    class ViewController: UIViewController {
2.        var player:AVAudioPlayer = AVAudioPlayer()
3.        var pausePlay:String = "Play"
```

4.   let audioPath =
NSBundle.mainBundle().pathForResource("Ocean_Waves", ofType: "mp3")!

Line 1 is unchanged from the way that Swift creates it when you first create the new project. In **Line 2,** we create variable named player of type AVAudioPlayer then set it equal to an empty (unitialized) audio player. In **Line 3** we create a variable called pausePlay which is a string and we set it's initial value to "Play".   **Line 4** is the most complicated of the whole application. Later in the application we'll start the AV player by passing it an mp3 file we wish it to play. The location of this file is expressed as a URL. Although you may think of a URL as a web address, it really stands for Universal Resource Locator and in this case we'll use it to locate the resource we want to load. So we are creating a constant (rather than a variable because it doesn't change) using the let command.

The constant is named *audioPath* and we are setting it equal to an internal resource in our project. **NSBundle** refers to the bundle of files included in your application. **mainBundle** means the directory where the current application executable is located. (This implies that you can use other places to locate your files and while true this is outside the scope of this book).

Next we call **pathForResource** which takes two parameters, the name of the file and the type of file.   Substitute the name of the mp3 file you selected.

Now we have an audio player and way to tell it which file we want played.

Add the Actions

Disable the slider control on start

You could just select the slider control and locate the properties box on the right of the screen and deselect Enabled or you could do this in code by adding it to the viewDidLoad event.

```
override func viewDidLoad() {
    super.viewDidLoad()
        self.sliderVolume.enabled = false
```

}

Code the Play/Pause Button

Control drag the button to the code window and create an action:

```
1.       @IBAction func buttonPush(sender: AnyObject) {
2.          if pausePlay=="Play"{
3.             playButton.setTitle ("Pause", forState: .Normal)
4.             do {
5.                try player = AVAudioPlayer(contentsOfURL:
NSURL(fileURLWithPath: audioPath))
6.                player.play()
7.                pausePlay = "Pause"
8.                self.sliderVolume.enabled = true
9.                return
10.            } catch{
11.            print ("Error loading the audio")
12.            }
13.         }
14.         if pausePlay=="Pause"{
15.            pausePlay = "Play"
16.            playButton.setTitle ("Play", forState: .Normal)
17.            player.pause ()
18.            return
19.         }
20.      }
```

Line 1 is created by xCode when you create the action. **Line 20** closes the action with the } symbol. Starting on **Line 2** there is an if condition which checks to see if the *pausePlay* variable is set to "Play". When the application first starts this condition will be true because that is what we set the initial value of the variable to hold. What it means is that the button says **Play**, and if we push it the music should play, rather than pause.

Once we push the play button, the first thing we'll want to do is set the button to display the word **Pause**, which we do on **Line 3**. This is because if the music is already playing, it makes no sense to continue to display a button that says play.

Next we'll begin to actually play the music. Because this process is error prone, and Swift knows it, it insists that this procedure be done inside a Try/Catch block. This starts on **Line 4** with the do statement. **Line 5** tries to load the audio file into the player. If it fails **Lines 10 – 12** will "catch" the problem and print out an error message. Assuming that the audio loaded properly, **Line 6** will tell the player to start playing. In **Line 7** we switch the value of the variable *pausePlay* to "Pause". This variable is used to keep track of whether to pause or play the music when the button is pressed. On Line 8 we enable the slider control to allow the user to adjust the volume.

This is a good idea because if the user adjusts the player volume before it has been initialized the app will crash so this easily avoided by only enabling the control once the player has successfully started.

Line 9 simply states **return**. This tells Swift not to continue in this function any further. Without this line the next statement would advance to the next line, which stop the player-- which is not what we want.

Beginning on **Line 14** we handle the case of what to do if the music is already playing and the user wants to pause it. **Line 15** switches the *pausePlay* variable so we know what to do the next time the function in invoked. **Line 16** changes the button text to read **Play** again and **Line 17** pause the music.

Adjusting the Volume

This is actually super simple because the slider control has a value from 0 to 1 and so does the AVPlayer volume level.

```
@IBAction func changeVolume(sender: AnyObject) {
    player.volume = sliderVolume.value
}
```

28

Submitting an app to the Apple App store

Introduction

Apple's app store is a tightly controlled environment. Apple wants to know how you are, what your application is supposed to do, and to ensure that it doesn't violate any of their terms of use and other guidelines.

Apple's guidelines are very complete and well thought out. The good news is that most of the guidelines are in plain English that a normal person can understand. For instance here's a typical element:

> If your App doesn't do something useful, unique or provide some form of lasting entertainment, or if your app is plain creepy, it may not be accepted.

You can find all of Apple's guidelines here:

https://developer.apple.com/app-store/review/guidelines/

What you Need

You need to be a member of the Apple developer program. You will also need screen shots in different sizes, an app icon, and icons for the store.

Get ready for Rejection

Apple typically rejects most of the application submissions that it gets and it is not unusual at all for your application to be initially rejects. Sometimes the issue is as simple as an auto-layout mistake that prevents the application from looking right on a specific device. You can expect to receive detailed information about why your application was rejected so that you can correct the issue and then re-submit it.

Launch Screen

Apple wants your launch screen to be dull so don't over do it.

Certificates and Identifiers

Your application must be signed by an Apple-issued certificate, even to run it on your own device. Xcode is the easiest way to request certificates. Simply connect your device to your Mac and click Use for Development in Xcode's organizer window.

Follow Along with Apple

Apple has documented the process extensively, and it seems silly to duplicate it again here since they can change their process at any time.

See
https://developer.apple.com/library/ios/documentation/IDEs/Conceptual/AppDistributionGuide/SubmittingYourApp/SubmittingYourApp.html

29

Conclusion

Wrapping it up

I hope by now you have gotten a good sense of the power of Swift and whether building iOS applications is for you.

Did this book cover everything there is to know about Swift? No, it sure didn't and I don't think any book ever will. Swift is a very rich topic and it is always improving and evolving. The point of this book was to start you on your way.

If I succeeded in giving you a taste of whether Swift is going to bring you joy, please take a moment and rate the book on Amazon. It really, really matters to helping the book stand out among the millions of books competing with it and helps me out quite a bit in writing continuously better books.

If there was something about this book that you didn't like, was factually incorrect, or could just be made **better**, please email me at alanforbes@outlook.com and I promise to write you back. The great thing about ebooks is that they are never officially done, and I always take constructive feedback to heart and upload fixes and corrections. Amazon automatically pushes these changes out to devices so your feedback could really help somebody. Thank you for reading my book!

-Alan

Internet Resources

Be sure to check out these great resources:

https://github.com/raywenderlich/swift-style-guide

http://jamesonquave.com/blog/developing-ios-apps-using-swift-tutorial/

Index

action..61

Action Segue...115

addition...13

Arrays...37

    Adding objects...38

    Inserting Items...39

    Joining..39

    Referencing objects...38

    Removing Items...39

    Subset..39

assignment operators...13

Assistant Editor..72

Auto Layout..56

AVFoundation...149

    AVAudioPlayer...149

    volume..152

Bar Button Item..122

Bool...9

Camel Casing...11

class...28

    computed property...34

    initialization...30

CLLocatonManagerDelegate...142

Cocoa...3, 52

Cocoa Touch..3, 52

Comments..8

comparison operators...19

Compound assignment operators...15

Core Location...

    CLLocationCoordinate2D...132

    CLLocationCoordinate2DMake..132

    CLLocationDegrees..132

    CLLocatonCoordinate2DMake...131

    core location (CL) framework..131

Core Location framework..139

debug window...78

Dictionary...41

    Adding Items..44

    count property...43

    Empty...42

isEmpty...43

Iterating..45

Removing Items...44

Subscript Syntax..43

division...13

do / try / catch...26

do...while loop...22

Double..9

Fixed Space Bar Button item...124

Flexible Space Bar Button Item...124

Float...9

for loop...19

for-in loop..20

Functions..46

"Throwing" An Error..48

guard statement...24

if statement..22

if..else statement...22

Image View control..84

Info.plist...141

iOS..52

isEmpty..17

Label...89

labels..66

let...8

Location Manager...142

    didUpdateLocations...146

    music..147

    startUpdatingLocation...145

Main.storyboard...64

MapKit...127

    GPS..139

    MKCoordinateRegion...132

    MKCoordinateRegionMake....................................132

    MKCoordinateSpan...132

    MKCoordinateSpanMake......................................131p.

    MKMapViewDelegate...130

    MKPointAnnotation...135

    region...130

    setRegion..133

MKCoordinateSpan..132

multiplication..13

music...147

Navigation Bar...117

NSBundle...150

    pathForResource...150

NSLocationAlwaysUsageDescription...142

NSLocationWhenInUseUsageDescription.......................................141

NSURL...108

NSURLRequest...109

NSUserDefaults..110

outlet..61

playground..5

print...11

project navigator...63

Segmented control...99

string...16

String Concatenation..14

subtraction...13

switch statement..23

ternary conditional operator..24

text field..67, 106

Toolbar...117

Type Inference...11

UIDatePicker control...94

UIGestureRecognizer...136

UILongPressGestureRecognizer..135

UISlider..89

UIWebControl...107

UIWebView control..105

User Interface Constraints...53

var...8

Visual Studio...60p.

while loop...21

Xcode...1, **4**